Natures Mirror

—Of—

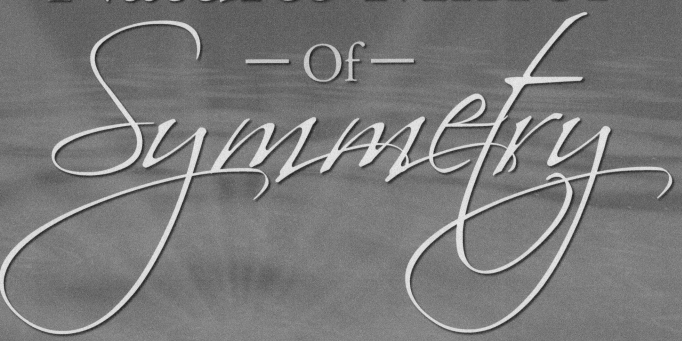

Symmetry

CHERYL CAINE

LitPrime
"Your story is our priority"

LitPrime Solutions
21250 Hawthorne Blvd
Suite 500, Torrance, CA 90503
www.litprime.com
Phone: 1 (209) 788-3500

Scripture quotations marked JB are from The Jerusalem Bible, copyright © 1966 by Darton, Longman & Todd, Ltd. and Doubleday, a division of Bantam Doubleday Dell Publishing Group, Inc. Reprinted by permission.

Published by LitPrime Solutions   06/04/2021

ISBN: 978-1-953397-62-1(sc)
ISBN: 978-1-953397-63-8(hc)
ISBN: 978-1-953397-64-5(e)

Any people depicted in stock imagery provided by iStock are models, and such images are being used for illustrative purposes only.

Certain stock imagery © iStock.

Contents

I will be donating 20% of the net proceeds from this book to environmental causes.

Introduction

I WAS ONE OF THOSE ENDANGERED species we hear about so often. That particular species is called the art teacher in the public school system, for first through sixth grade. I was called "the artist in residence," which is a very cheap way for schools to still have an art teacher, without having to pay a contracted salary for one. I was doing it for free, and the only way I could afford to do it was because I had just become retired, so I could volunteer my time. This was my gift to the children in my community who had a passion for art, and a need for opportunities to use their imaginations and be creative.

Art as a subject in school, is considered expendable, and therefore the first thing dropped from the regular curriculum. My payment was watching the students come up with creations that they were proud of, and seeing their eyes widen with imagination and their jaws drop in amazement when I showed them new ways of seeing and appreciating nature. I soon realized that I was introducing many of them to the wonders of nature for the first time. I was connecting them to the greatest inspiration and source of life we have.

William Blake writes, "Nature is imagination itself." Albert Einstein tells us to "look deeply into Nature, and there you will understand everything better." We can't leave nature out of our children's big picture if we want our children to evolve in a balanced, healthy, and creative way. We can't put all the emphasis on technology, or they will lose their inheritance as human beings on this planet.

I found that most children have lost their sense of wonder and are surprisingly skeptical by the time they reach the third grade. I enjoyed blowing their minds as they learned to see nature in ways that made them feel like they were "Dorothy of Oz" just landing in Munchkinland.

I started my first classes by asking the children, "Where does one go to get inspiration and ideas for art?" They raised their hands and said things like books, teachers, and other artists. I suggested they were leaving out the most important source of all. Finally, I had to come out and say to them, "How about Mother Nature?" Not one child in two different schools thought of this—not one!

Oh my, we have neglected this wisdom so completely! Our children are bereft. I would daresay they have been orphaned when they have no reference at all for Mother Nature. One child raised her hand and corrected me by saying that "it was not Mother Nature, it's God!" I learned then that to even mention Mother Nature in public school, was being politically incorrect. What a shame!

I realized through this teaching experience, just how suppressed and totally dismissed the feminine presence known as "Mother Nature" and "Mother Earth", has become in the modern psyche. She has now been delegated to words like *landscape*, *outdoors*, or, even worse, the *gross natural product*. Carl Jung said once, "You can throw Mother Nature out with a pitchfork, but she will always come back." We may think we have put her in her place, but we need to remember that she has the last word.

As nature is going unnoticed, we are replacing her with cell phones, tablets, and computers. It is the imbalance of our age. Perhaps we are experiencing the long-term effects of the Inquisition that labeled those who honored Mother Nature, as witches, and burned them at the stake. So many "first peoples" around the world have experienced the harsh cruelty and suppression of this kind of mentality. I also think of Cat Stevens's song "Where Do the Children Play?" I rarely see children playing outdoors, unless it is an organized sport.

Since I am writing my own book, I am grateful I still have the freedom of speech to express my heart and mind and draw attention to what I think is sadly being left out of our collective values. In my book, I will honor Mother Nature as the divine feminine, who, along with the divine masculine, is in everything. It is time once again for there to be the wholeness that acknowledges the "Spirit in Matter." This includes both the masculine and feminine. The closer I look at nature, the more hermaphroditic it appears to be. I will try to show you how this is so. I will challenge you to not just look at the pictures I am showing you, *but study them and look deeply into them as Einstein would have advised.*

The artists, poets, and craftsman of old knew this. Ralph Waldo Emerson writes, "Nature will always wear the colors of the Spirit in Nature." In this modern age, we may have forgotten this. If that is the case, we have been blinded. We have to first realize that we are out of balance, and this imbalance is destroying us. We need our minds, and hearts renewed if we are to have our eyes opened again.

I am encouraged by the science of physics because it uses terms like *"lost symmetry"* and *"the hidden third"*, which I find to be such an important part of really seeing nature. You will be amazed to see how symmetry reveals the "hidden third" in everything. I am not sure where the science of physics will go, but I think it is a science that is open to experience. I hope that these scientists are generous with what they learn. I think they will realize that there is a hidden soul and spirit in nature that we have ignored for too long. I just hope they will honor it, not just tamper with it.

Jungian psychology is another science that has given us maps and understanding into our own human nature that, before was unavailable to us. I will refer to this and share my process looking into the mirror of my own soul, which is another way of seeing in symmetry.

I will talk about how the divine feminine, is drawing closer to us at this time, reminding us of her presence in this time in-between ages. She wants to give us her wisdom and help us in our process of healing, birthing, and evolving. Our conscious egos will have to learn to be in service of the evolution we need to make.

I am hoping this book will give you some tools, to move forward, and accept Her challenge.

CHAPTER 1

Unless You Become as a Little Child

I T ALL STARTED WITH A very plain Christmas tree in the lobby of my bank. While I waited in line to cash my check, I noticed that their Christmas tree was decorated with nothing but plain white cards. Being curious, before I left, I went over and checked out these cards. They were requests for Christmas presents from a boarding school, for at-risk children in our community. I read a number of these requests and decided I would get some of these gifts.

I was surprised to see that in several of these requests, the children asked for a "mask-making kit." I thought this was a unique request, particularly since each child could only ask for one gift. I took these requests and set out to find them a "mask-making kit."

I have been a craftsperson by trade. I made dental crowns and bridges, and full mouth reconstruction for a living. This was when everything was done by hand, without computers. I was good with my hands and enjoyed my craft. In my free time, I had made many masks myself. I could not imagine a kit being as much fun as creating a mask of my own, but I began looking for a kit for these kids. Maybe this was the latest thing that kids wanted, so I thought it would be easy to find. I looked in department stores, craft stores, art supply stores, toy stores, and everywhere I could think of, but I could not find anything close to a mask-making kit. All the time I was searching, a little voice in my head was saying, *"You could teach them yourself. You know how to do it." That would be much more fun than a kit.* I finally called the school and offered my services to come and teach them mask making. I thought, *there might be more kids -who would enjoy making a mask too.* The secretary took my name and phone number, and I waited for a reply.

Christmas came and went, but I did not hear from them. The idea to do this for the children, had latched onto me though, and I thought about it often. I kept telling myself that I had offered, but they did not call back, so what could I do?

Near the end of January, I was at my workbench at work, and my regular radio station was getting poor reception that morning, so I switched to another station. This station was broadcasting interviews with local artists, and these artists had a project going where they would show lay people how to express themselves through art. It captured my attention, so I started to listen.

At the end of the interview, the radio station opened the air to questions and comments from the radio audience. I normally would never do this kind of thing, especially since I was at work, but since I was alone in the office at the time, I got up and called in. I told them about the Christmas tree and the unusual requests from the children, and then finally my desire to teach them mask making. The artists were all encouraging me to go for it!

When I hung up the phone, I sat back down at my bench again and listened as other people called in. I was taken back because these callers were all responding to my call, and telling me to go for it as well. Grade school teachers called in to say they had no art program in their schools and did not feel qualified to teach art themselves. They would so welcome something like this.

Oh my it was then I realized that I had just told the whole metro area about this project I wanted to do with the children, and they heard it. It felt like I had just been given an assignment from my higher Self and the voice in my head said, *"You can do this."* Tuning this out was no longer an option. I told my higher Self to help make a way for me, and I would do it. I knew then that this would happen.

In early February, I went to a concert with a friend, and in the intermission, my friend ran into someone she had gone to college with. Her friend mentioned she was now working at the very school I had offered to teach at. She immediately had my attention, and once again, I told my story about the offer I had made. She said there was only one person to present my offer to, and she gave me his name and address at the school. A way was being made.

I wrote my letter and got an immediate response. They asked me to come to the school and show them my ideas, which I did. These were children with special needs, and I got a lot of guidelines and restrictions about what kind of masks I could have them make and the materials we could use. I set out gathering these materials. I even had my beauty shop saving hair for us to use. I gathered these materials as diligently as a squirrel getting ready for winter.

It was a number of months until finally, I got the opportunity to have the classes. I found out later that they had to do a background check on me and do some special arranging to make this happen. There were kids in the class ranging from age twelve to age seventeen. We had a series of three class sessions of one and a half hours each. It was plenty of time for them to make a good mask and enjoy it.

My reward came when one of the boy's asked me to glue-gun his mask to a stick so he could hold it up and "dance to his best music with it." I glued it for him and handed it back. Immediately, he started dancing because his best music was already in his head. As he danced, he sang, "I can't wait to show my mom, and I can't wait to show my best friend." In my heart, I was dancing with him.

I had gathered all these teaching materials and had thought of some different ideas using symmetry, so what was I going to do with all this material now? I called the community grade school that was only about four blocks from my house and offered to teach mask making to their fifth and sixth graders, free of charge. They gladly accepted, and I gave them the same three sessions of one and a half hours for each class. By the last session I was known in the school as the "masked lady."

As I packed up my materials to go, I wondered if this was it now. Just then one of the first-grade teachers came in and asked me if I could possibly come up with a project for the first and second graders. I was hesitant at first because I did not know then the creativity first graders are capable of. We blew each other's minds. There is no one more creative than a first grader in my mind, and they are not hesitant about expressing it.

Of course, I could not leave out the third and fourth graders, so they were next. It was at this time that I had one of those full-circle moments. I was pushing my cart of materials down the hall on my way to one of the last sessions when a boy from the class I was going to looked out the back door and saw me coming. He shouted to the class, "She's coming!"

I instantly remembered myself at his age, seeing my art teacher coming down the hall and my heart leaping for joy. I had been in his shoes when I was his age. Now here I was, the teacher this time.

When I was through with this project, I had taught the whole school. I felt like it was my school too now. I learned as much as the children had, perhaps more. One of the ideas I had developed during this process was the use of symmetry. I had found an in-depth way of looking at and seeing nature that had never occurred to me before. This was a whole new phenomenon that had opened up to me, and Mother Nature was my teacher and the children's teacher too.

I know that if I had not taken up this challenge with these kids and not "become as a little child" myself, I would not have learned or been able to share with you this amazing world found in symmetry.

CHAPTER 2

Nature's Amazing Mirror of Symmetry

"This beautiful physical form merely hints at something more beautiful and much greater, which is hidden in it." Gerd Ziegler's "Tarot: Mirror of the Soul"

WITH MY BOOK, I WILL try to reveal through the use of the mirror of symmetry what is hidden from us but truly greater than what our eyes can normally see. These are reflections of the divine that is all around us but forgotten because we do not see it. There are reoccurring patterns that are archetypal and sacred in nature. They run throughout nature, including ourselves, even though we have started to think that somehow we are above and outside of nature. This is one of the biggest dangers of our age.

When I started working in symmetry with my pictures, I had a Photo-shop software that could turn my photos into four-fold symmetry. By this, I mean all four sides of my pictures were placed reflectively on all four sides. As I was seeing this for the first time, it just looked like an elaborate wallpaper design. It wasn't until I started to crop these designs and study them separately that I began to see distinct themes in these patterns. It was like a door had opened to a whole new dimension.

Barbara Walker, in her book *"The Woman's Encyclopedia of Myths and Secrets,"* tells us how powerful mirror reflections were in the imagination of the ancients. She says, "Because of the universal belief that one's reflection is a vital part of one's soul, mirrors and other reflective surfaces were long regarded as soul catchers or doorways to the other world of spirits."

There are many stories in mythology that talk about these encounters with our own reflection and the reflection of the divine in some way. I think of the hero Perseus, who killed the "terrible Gorgon" that could turn men into stone. He was able to do this by looking at Medusa through a mirror reflection. I find it interesting that after he did this, he himself took on some of the outward wild hair appearance of the Gorgon himself. This showed that an integration was happening that his heroic journey had given him. He now knew more about himself, and he was more whole.

I think of the story of Narcissus, the god who died as he gazed at and pined for his own reflection in a reflecting pool. This was part of a death-and-rebirth drama that cyclically has always taken place in nature, but it can happen in ourselves too.

The goddesses Maya and Sophia were thought of as the "creators of these reflections and of the spiritual reality

3

in this mirror hidden from us within the material world." Maya was also the "goddess of earthly appearances and illusions" who actually prevents us from seeing into this hidden dimension.

This is hard to understand until we remember that consciousness is a choice and we have to deliberately seek it out. Hermann Hesse wrote that "Every phenomenon on earth is an image and all images are open gates through which the soul can enter the inner world when it is ready."

Maya and Sophia were virgin goddesses, and they were both considered the mother of the "Enlightened One." Maya was "the mother of Hermes, the wise hermaphrodite as the "Enlightened One." In Buddhist tradition, she was the "virgin mother of the Buddha," who is also an "Enlightened One." Even though the virgin Mary has been presented in different ways over the centuries, she is part of this archetypal pattern as the virgin mother of Jesus, the "Enlightened One." We will see more on this later in the book.

Zimmer called her "Maya-Shakti," "the world-protecting feminine of the "Ultimate Being." Just this description makes me awestruck. "She represents the spontaneous and loving acceptance of this tangible reality of ours." She dwells on the borderline of our soul's journey, inspiring, protecting, nourishing, and admonishing us as we brave our own process to enlightenment. She is the one who can help us cocreate our lives and give us meaning. We will see her again in the chapter on "Spider Woman." This is the same archetype with another name given to her by a different culture.

Different chapters will show some of these different archetypes and how they appear in nature and in our own lives. Being aware of this hidden dimension can help us become more conscious of nature and our own lives. This is necessary if we are to evolve in human consciousness. With these plates, I will show you how I found these patterns in my pictures and worked with them to become conscious of them, and how they might work in my own life.

PLATE 1 CHAPTER 2

"Making order out of chaos"— Newspaper Rock, Arizona.

PLATE 1 CHAPTER 2 of petroglyphs on a cliff wall in Arizona was completely full of symbols, and messages that looked like a conglomeration of messages from the past. It may have been a newspaper to the ancients, but it was Greek to me. When I put this image into four-fold symmetry, there appeared a beautiful organized set of designs which made four separate design patterns. It is actually eight-fold because you can turn this on its side and see these patterns from another angle as well. All these patterns have clues to the four-fold nature of life. Each of the four designs is another part of the whole.

Since I was coming at this from the standpoint of an artist, I was looking for the aesthetic at first, but soon, it became apparent that there were recognizable patterns, and they were symbolic of different parts of the whole. I started to discover what these designs might represent. Then I started to categorize them, picking out the different themes in these patterns. They are like sacred geometry when they are placed in symmetry like this. These patterns are there, no matter what picture you use. I found they actually showed an aspect of the divine that is being expressed in this picture. I found that to understand these pictures, I needed the help of mythology and the wisdom of older cultures as well as, psychology and alchemy. Modern explanations were not sufficient. This was an eye-opener to what is missing in the present modern age. We have lost the meaning, sacredness, and the power of the symbolic in everything.

I would like to caution anyone who is thinking of taking pictures and putting them into symmetry just for the fun of it and getting carried away in the process. This is truly an archetypal dimension with a life of its own. When you put these images in to symmetry, it is almost like they see you as well as you see them. One becomes responsible for understanding them. It is almost like being on a pilgrimage, and you must now discover what is being shown and how it pertains to you. I could also say it is like an initiation that takes you into your depths.

In this process, you learn it is not all about ego consciousness. It's about allowing your ego to become conscious. This is the process of making order out of chaos.

In this transition between ages that we are in, this is an important role that our egos can play in finding our way. Let's start to dissect these patterns and see what they reveal.

PLATE 2 CHAPTER 2

"Tree of life."

PLATE 2 CHAPTER 2 came from a four-fold picture of a beautiful garden in Hawaii. I liken it to paradise. Here, I have cut out two adjacent sections of the four, and when I look at them together, they look like a cross that can make a connection to the heavens like a tree of life. This is the sacred center that can balance all things. In my imagination, the orchids are like the Pleiades star cluster that is in the heavens. The cross is the process we go through as we become conscious. It is also the fulfilling of the promise that can take us to a higher level.

PLATE 3 CHAPTER 2

"Mother Earth enthroned."

Here, we see the soul of our Mother Earth enthroned with the sun disk at her center. To find this, I took one section of a four-fold picture and cut it out. **PLATE 3 CHAPTER 2** is from the four-corners area of the American Southwest. She shows us her connection with the first peoples of this area who still hold her lovingly in their heart and soul, by wearing the moccasins worn by the woman of this area.

As in so many images of Mother Earth, her face is partially hidden or masked. There is a timeless quality in her face though, and to me, she appears to be crying. The divine aspect of the feminine comes up in some form or another in every four-fold picture. This one is one of my favorites.

PLATE 4 CHAPTER 2

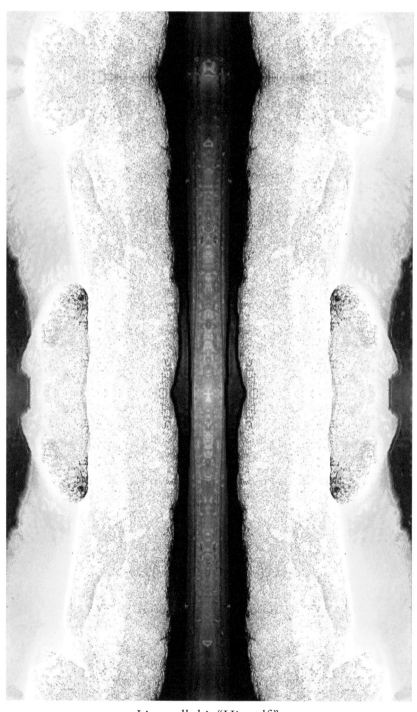

I just call this "Himself."

This is the masculine aspect also seen somewhere in every four-fold picture. He is always seen with a pillar, rod, sword, or scepter, representing the phallus. Sometimes he is a charioteer, and sometimes a king.

This always appears in relation to the feminine chalice. **PLATE 4 CHAPTER 2**, the chalice is at the top, and the scepter goes through it. We get a small glimpse of his head at the top of this scepter in lapis blue. Lapis was sacred to the divine feminine.

At the bottom, I see very subtly in the center, his knees, as if he is seated or possibly enthroned. He might be a sun king because I see the pyramids of the sun on the sides. In this picture he is glowing like the sun.

PLATE 5 CHAPTER 2

"The sun kings and the sun."

The sun in **PLATE 5 CHAPTER 2** is in the center. Every four-fold picture has the sun in it somewhere. It reminds me of the previous picture of Mother Earth with the sun in her center. It shows us that the sun is the center of our earthly life. We revolve around it and it gives us light. The sun has been associated in many cultures with two solstice kings and sun pyramids.

I am not surprised to see these solar kings, one on top and the other on the bottom. The king who is on top appears to be the ascending, victorious one. I found it interesting to see his phallus coming out of his head with wings as if ascending above the clouds. This could relate to awakening consciousness or ascension after resurrection. The grail of the masculine aspect is found in the head. One can birth something from the head that is being awakened, and give it life.

Below, we see the phallus like the healing symbol of a caduceus with wings and the sun disk on top. The wings of this phallus appear like butterfly wings from this direction. This is the down-under sun that awaits rejuvenation in the womb of the feminine aspect. I think of the description of Christ, as coming "with healing in his wings." About an inch up from the bottom we see a butterfly, representing the transformation that is taking place. We see another chalice with the heads of two doves on either side. This shows the feminine and hermaphroditic nature of this image.

When we turn this on its side, we see the pyramids, and a large outline of a scarab in the center. This is the scarab aspect that pushes up the sun. The scarab is helping in the birth of consciousness. I will talk about the scarab later in the book.

PLATE 6 CHAPTER 2

"The womb of Spider Woman".

When I cut one of these four sections in half again, the pixel quality is lost. We can still see and make out what is being portrayed here though. **PLATE 6 CHAPTER 2** was a picture taken of a spiderweb, so it is not surprising to see the womb of Spider Woman as she weaves life within herself. In the very center, we see the chalice and the sword, as the coming together of opposites.

I see faintly two sets of legs behind this chalice and sword. It appears in my imagination like the legs of the feminine in front and the masculine behind her. Again, we can see them coming together. This is happening all around us everywhere in a beautiful way.

Around what appears to be her ovaries, we see what looks like two doves, which is so often seen at the top of the chalice along with two snakes. I see a dance going on too. This is the dance of life.

We will see much more of Spider Woman later in the book. We will see more of the doves and the snakes and the chalice too because they are in everything.

PLATE 7 CHAPTER 2

"Fall foliage without symmetry."

PLATE 7 CHAPTER 2 shows us how limited our one-dimensional sight is and how surprising and even startling it can be when we finally see it in symmetry. This plate has not been placed in symmetry. We will see for ourselves that what is hiding from the viewpoint of symmetry, is so much greater than what we see ordinarily.

PLATE 7 CHAPTER 2 on its own is not too remarkable. It is a picture I took of fall foliage. I remember asking myself as I took this picture, why am I taking a picture of this? When I put it into symmetry, I found out why.

PLATE 8 CHAPTER 2

"The golden scarab pushed up the sun".

PLATE 8 CHAPTER 2 truly shows us how the hidden third center can show us so much more than our eyes can see. Here is the glowing golden scarab pushing up out of the dense dark prima materia underneath it. Materia is matter - the mother, and the scarab is trapped in this matter and must push upwards to release the sun of consciousness. The Egyptians called him the "Holy ball roller."

In alchemy, this third dimension hidden from us, is where the base material came from, that they gathered and then needed to refine into gold. We will talk more about this process within ourselves in the chapter on the scarab.

We are not talking about literal gold, literal chalices or grails, literal swords, or literal scarabs. These are symbols of something much deeper within all of nature and ourselves. These are symbols that the ancients could truly relate to. Somehow, we got stuck on the material one dimensional aspect and ignored the spiritual, psychological, and symbolic. This is the real quest.

When you are not afraid to look into the mirror of your soul, and work with the symmetry you are shown there, you can begin on the road to becoming a cocreator of your destiny. If you are being called to do this work, the timing is right. Even for the collective, I can sense a readiness to begin this leap of consciousness. It can't be too soon because truly, we need to rise and take ourselves to higher ground. Like Stevie Wonder's song "Higher Ground," I feel like "it won't be too long."

CHAPTER 3

The In-between Time and the Goddess of Love and Wisdom

I HAD A DREAM THAT I was in a little coastal town overlooking the sea. It was very early in the morning and still dark. Everything about this dream was on the borderline of the in-between time.

I was walking up the sidewalk, and I stepped into a café for breakfast. There was an older woman at the counter who seemed to own the place. She was in the process of serving breakfast to the fishermen before they went out to sea. They too were on the borderline. I noticed that when they sat down at the counter, she greeted them like family and knew without asking, what their order would be. She was like a nurturing mother for adults. I could tell that they knew she cared about them, and that was why they were there.

She looked up and saw me as I was looking around for a place to sit down. She exclaimed, "Cheryl, you're here!" Then she said to everyone, "I want to introduce my daughter, Cheryl."

I was surprised because I had never seen her before. Her greeting felt so good though that I went along with it. I felt grateful to be considered her daughter. She dropped everything and took me in the back, where she said she had something for me. She handed me a statue, and I knew it was a special gift. I felt so loved and grateful, but I could hardly believe what was happening. Then I woke up.

The in-between times in our lives can be times when we receive unexpected gifts that we normally have no reference for. It can be a gift that is yet to be realized, like an opportunity or a talent that is latent, yet about to become a part of your life in a special way. It might be something that points to a future time. Now you can be aware when it does come and be ready to take full advantage of it. It will be like a light bulb moment that confirms your path when the time is right. For me, these are the gifts of Sophia, goddess of love and wisdom. She can appear to everyone in a different way, and she meets you where you are. Like the fishermen she was serving, she knows the moment you step into her in-between space who you are, and what you need to help you on your way, to fulfill your destiny. Everyone who comes into her space is her daughter or son.

Her appearance in your life presents itself at an appropriate time, even if you are not yet cognizant of her significance. It's a situation where you do not know her yet, but she knows you. She is not just present; she is giving you her blessing.

When I woke up, I wrote this dream down with a sense of wonder. It was still fresh in my mind when a few days later, I was on my way to lunch and walked by this handmade clothing store. There in the window was a bolt of this beautiful turquoise material that looked like a monochromatic oriental cloisonné design. I was so taken by this material, I went into the shop and asked the woman about the material, and what the design in it was. The woman must have thought my question was strange because she looked at me and said, "It isn't a message from God," and she did not know what the design was!

Her response was rather startling to me, but if she hadn't said it in this particular way, I would not have thought what came into my mind next, which was *Then it must be a message from the goddess*. I asked the woman to make me a dress jacket from this material. Now whenever I wore this jacket, I was reminded of the dream of the "woman by the sea" in the café. It became a concrete confirmation in real time, of something that happened in the dreamtime.

It helps to have something to carry over into real time, that you experience in this more allusive in-between time. Like all dreams, you can forget their impact and let it slip away. Important dreams should be remembered. Every time I wore that jacket, I was reminded that she was my mother.

The in-between time can be a very difficult time too. It is also a time of disorientation, uncertainty, and hard lessons. You may be going through a hard transition in your life, and her encouragement will be a welcome thing as your endurance is being tested. One needs to have discipline and determination to get through these trials. Mother Wisdom disciplines the ones she loves. You can't be half asleep or carelessly drifting during these difficult times in your life. She knows what you will be facing though, and how much you can endure. She is there to help see you though.

It was a very hard in-between time when I had another experience. I was struggling to find a new direction for my life after a particularly trying time. My husband and I had spent about four years taking care of my elderly in-laws. Caregiving for the elderly is not an easy responsibility. It requires devotion and patience. It's not like caring for someone who is convalescing, where the person is expected to improve and eventually get back to normal again. For the end-of-life caregiver, it's a life on hold. You give all your care and energy to someone you love, and in the end, you experience the loss. I was feeling so totally depleted that it was hard to think about starting in a new direction. It was an in-between time because one chapter of my life was over, and the next chapter had not yet begun. I did not even know where to start.

It was in this space that I got art materials together in my basement studio and got ready to make a mandala. Mandalas are a wonderful tool for helping one sort themselves out in these transitional times. Mandalas that are coming out of your soul take your irrational, instinctual side, and your intuition and mix them together to create a symbolic rendition of your life and process in that moment. This is significant in helping you heal, from a disorientating or fragmented time. Carl Jung used mandalas for himself and his patients to help bring order back into their lives. It brings us back into our center and helps us start again.

With tears in my eyes, I got ready to start this project. I can remember this moment as if I am looking down on myself with love. I think Mother Wisdom gives me this perspective. I put on Van Morrison's CD *"Beautiful Vision"* and began by dancing a mandala. I started dancing to the song "Dweller on the Threshold." This is a great song for the in-between times we go through. Sometimes the body has something to say too, and it can't be excluded. When it came to the song "Beautiful Vision," I said a little prayer for help in this process. Then I started my mandala.

I was on my own this weekend, so I worked on this project nonstop. I do not even remember stopping to eat. When I finished, I placed my mandala on a shelf to dry and let the wet paint and glue set. Then I sat down in my chair like I had finished a marathon. As I sat there, I did in fact, literally have a beautiful vision.

Before me stood this veiled, luminous, matronly figure in a beautiful turquoise blue gown with an oriental cloisonné print on it. Of course, it reminded me of my jacket material, but hers was much more elegant. She wore a massive pearl necklace of many strands, and they glowed around her neck. Her necklace was so bright and beautiful, it took my breath away.

She walked over to the shelf where I had laid my mandala, and she picked it up and held it to her heart. Then she placed it down and came back in front of me and started to make gestures with her hands. She pointed to one section of the room where there were shelves of accumulated materials for projects I had made in my teaching days with the children. She motioned for me to get rid of everything, including the large shelf.

So often, you have to let go of the old before something new can come in. She gestured for me to make a sacred space for myself, to have an altar and a meditative place to just be in my center. She did not make a sound and only communicated in gestures and through my thoughts. I understood completely what she was telling me. When the vision began to fade, I knew exactly what I needed to do to begin this transition.

When my husband came home from his trip, he was surprised to see me hauling out all this accumulated stuff and throwing it in the back of our pickup truck to haul to the dump. It took three trips to the dump to clear out this space, but it felt so good when it was done.

My next project was to make an altar for this new space. My new heart-dove mandala was hung in the very center, right above the fireplace. It became the mystic centering symbol for my new sacred space. This was the start of the next phase of my spiritual life. This space was where I could consciously attend wisdom. It was this mandala that made the connection for me between my real time and my dreamtime, and it truly made it my sacred space.

PLATE 1 CHAPTER 3

My "heart dove mandala".

That night when I went to bed, the mandala I had just made became another vision on my ceiling, with the heart glowing in the center. The little hearts I had sprinkled around the periphery of this mandala were presented to me one by one. I knew I was loved.

It felt like an olive branch had been passed to me like the one the dove had given to Noah to let him know that the waters of a difficult time were receding. Even though I was still in my depths, there was love, a promise, and a place to heal. It was a heart connection to the divine feminine in myself. I can sing along with Van Morrison every time I hear his song "Beautiful Vision"— "Stay with me all of the time." If you have never heard this song, go on YouTube and listen to it. It might help take you into your sacred space.

I would also recommend, if you can, to make a little space in your home or apartment, even if it is just an alcove or breezeway space, where you can honor and be reminded of this in-between time. It is too easy to be distracted and ignore this place of the "still-small voice of the Self." This is a place where you can get a good meal before you have to go out to sea. She is waiting at the boarder, when you show up, to remind you that you too are her daughter, or son. It is a place where you can put the concrete real-time symbols and images that come out of the dreamtime, and bring them together in symmetry within yourself, so you know you are truly on your path and attending wisdom.

CHAPTER 4

Mother Earth Is Crying, Have You Seen Her Tears?

"What are you becoming? What is this great Mother Earth dreaming as she turns slowly in her slumber? This dark night seems to never end, and when will she wake one morning and shrug her shoulders of sleep and wonder and become angry because the bones of her body are being torn apart cell by cell?"

"And what of that dark night within each of us that we cannot learn but to be broken like an arrow as her great back will be broken if we do not awaken with her?" Agnes Whistling Elk, from the book Flight of the Seventh Moon by Lynn Andrews.

THESE ARE THE WORDS OF a shamaness, whose life was spent listening to Mother Earth and honoring her. She was a wise woman of the first peoples of Canada. These first peoples around the world have honored her tears like few of the dominant cultures have. It is time everyone learned to see and honor her tears and wake up from their slumber.

PLATE 1 CHAPTER 4

"The totem pole".

Traveling though British Columbia, Canada, I came across this totem pole. One of the guides we had on this trip had explained that the figures on the bottom of the totem pole were the most important, and the most revered. The top of the pole was where the figures of lesser importance were. This is the opposite of our dominant culture's way of thinking.

The bottom figure on this totem pole is Mother Earth crying. These peoples have known that we have been in a dark night and our Mother Earth is crying. What happened to the rest of us? I hope we are starting to wake up, because as the quote implies, we need to. We are getting a message from our Mother Earth that it's time to do right! What is happening now is unsustainable, and we can't afford to be in denial.

Times of awakening can be a real trial and even perilous if we do not get the message. The consequences of this awakening have already been felt, in fact it feels like the other shoe has dropped and these warnings are no longer warnings, but new realities. To put a new twist on an older quote, it is time to ask not what Mother Nature can do for you but rather what you can do for Mother Nature. It's time for her to be in that revered place at the bottom of all our totem poles now.

Gandhi challenged us to consider our needs not our wants. Some of us will have to tighten our belts and change our habits so that our children can have a better life. The myth of domination over nature has truly run amuck. We need to make new priorities now, or how will we explain this mess to our children? If we don't, our rainbow of hope and promise for the future will be lost. Since it has taken us so long to open our eyes, we may be in for some real ordeals. There are consequences for our unconscious behavior, and the longer we ignore it, the louder the messages become.

I have seen one wonderful nature program after another leave us with the same message. We all have heard it—we have to change, and time is running out. I was surprised when I went to a taco place for lunch and the walls were all decorated with displays of the many endangered species of animals around the world. This is what our children have realized as normal. This is the wallpaper of their lives. This would have been unheard of when I was a child. How is this affecting their hearts and minds?

We have so completely encroached on the habitat of Earth's creatures that I am finding it interesting to see wild animals starting to encroach on our lives now. In places we never used to see them, whole herds of elk, one hundred strong, have moved in on coastal towns in Oregon. They eat the people's landscaping, like it is a smorgasbord laid out just for them. People who are not used to dealing with wild animals are having town hall meetings to learn how to deal with these wild animals and the dangers that come when interacting with them. These wild animals are just trying to survive now in our world.

There are nice new marina docks leading out to people's boats that are now being blocked by huge noisy sea lions. When they are through sunning themselves, they compete for the fisherman's fish and literally pull fish right off their lines. It's like they are saying, "This is what it feels like people." They used to be out of sight and out of mind, to where we had to go to special places to look for them. This too was unnatural.

One of the first things people began to think of is "Euthanize these animals." There are laws on the books that prevent this from happening,—but for how long? Are we going to literally make war on wildlife now? This is happening for a reason, and we need to find out what it is and make changes that include habitat for the wildlife.

When nature is treated like an inconvenient nuisance, we know we are out of touch. It's time to look in the mirror and see what our role is in this imbalance. We have ignored the concerned scientists for decades. Now we are living with smoke-filled summers, global warming, and its record-breaking heat, with extreme weather of all kinds.

Environmental impact statements should mean something, but they are being ignored, suppressed, or bought off. Our young people are the ones who will have to pick up the slack of what we have neglected for too long. Our politics have been self-serving and shortsighted. What we have forgotten is that Mother Nature has her own form of justice.

I have a number of pictures that I have taken that show our Mother Earth in tears. It's not just an image on a totem pole. Some of these pictures are not in symmetry, so they can only be seen when we look at them in profile. Looking at nature in profile is one way of seeing what is usually hidden from us. Other pictures, we will see through the mirror of symmetry, so we can see for ourselves what we have not been able to see otherwise.

"Mother Earth crying out"

PLATE 2 CHAPTER 4 in profile, facing the right, shows her radiating face. Her mouth seems to be slightly open, as if crying out. I can see her tears falling down the side of her face. This picture comes from the four-corners area of the American Southwest.

PLATE 3 CHAPTER 4

"Mother nature on the beach"

PLATE 3 CHAPTER 4 was taken on a beach along the Oregon Coast. In profile, she is facing left wearing a blue dress with a reddish-brown veil. You can see clearly the tears coming down her cheeks. They seem to glisten in the sun.

PLATE 4 CHAPTER 4

"Mother nature with her Dove Crying".

PLATE 4 CHAPTER 4 facing left shows her with her with her totem, the dove. Both are facing left. I can see her tears as she seems to be trying to cry out. This too is from the American Southwest.

PLATE 5 CHAPTER 4

"Mother as the wise woman crying".

PLATE 5 CHAPTER 4 taken in New Mexico shows her in her crone phase, facing right. I can almost picture her as if she is just waking up and there are tears coming down her cheeks. When I look at it closely, I can see a masculine figure right next to her who also appears to be crying. Perhaps this is the divine masculine next to her.

PLATE 6 CHAPTER 4

"Mother nature is in mourning"

PLATE 6 CHAPTER 4 is also from New Mexico. This is the picture I used on my book cover. Mother Earth here appears tired and weary, like she has been crying for some time. I can see a tear on her lips. In profile, she appears very sad. She is facing left.

PLATE 7 CHAPTER 4

"Southwest crying Mother nature."

PLATE 7 CHAPTER 4 from the Southwest shows her in profile facing left. She looks down, and tears are coming down her face. Some of these images are very subtle, so you have to be looking for them to find them, but they are everywhere.

PLATE 8 CHAPTER 4

"Mother Earths mask".

PLATE 8 CHAPTER 4 placed in symmetry shows her masked, yet through it, we can still see her tears coming down. The center of this mask reminds me of the column Egyptians called the *djed*. This is the ladder like image that represented the backbone of the dying and resurrecting god. This was how the god's life was renewed. Interestingly enough, this *djed* was sometimes pictured topped by the feathers of Ma'at. Ma'at is the Egyptian name for the Great Mother-goddess. The feathers of Ma'at are not seen on her headdress here from this angle, but if you turn it upside down, and put it in reverse, the sides of the mask appear like the feathers of Ma'at. These are the feathers of truth and justice.

Ma'at was the goddess who personified the mother of truth and justice. Her laws governed all. Her justice was justice for all. Even the gods were governed by her laws. I found in Barbara Walker's book *"The Woman's Encyclopedia of Myths and Secrets"*, a confession made to Ma'at. She writes,

> "I have not been a man of anger. I have done no evil to mankind. I have not inflicted pain. I have made none to weep. I have done violence to no man. I have not done harm unto animals. I have not robbed the poor. I have not fouled water. I have not trampled fields. I have not behaved with insolence. I have not judged hastily. I have not stirred up strife. I have not made any man to commit murder

for me. I have not stolen land. I have not cheated in measuring the bushel. I have allowed no man to suffer hunger. I have not increased my wealth except with such things as are my own possessions. I have not seized wrongfully the properties of other. I have not taken milk from the mouths of babes".

This was the nature of the laws of Ma'at. In Samaria, she was known also as the "womb" and the "underworld." This makes this mask of the crying goddess very interesting. The divine feminine is in a time of sorrowful sojourning because her laws and her values have been lost. This too could explain her tears.

PLATE 9 CHAPTER 4

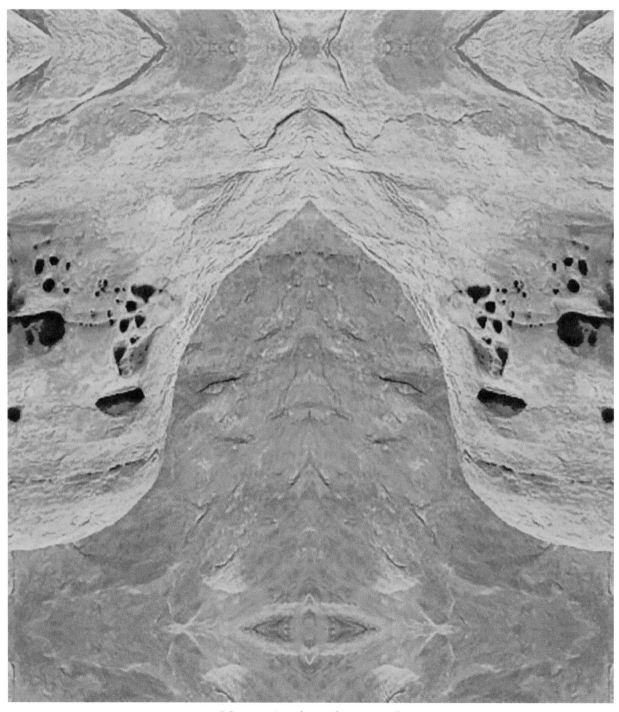

"Canyon Lands mother crying"

PLATE 9 CHAPTER 4 placed in symmetry is from Canyon Lands, Utah. We can clearly see her tears. The faces on either side of her seem to be looking on in shock and sympathy. Reversed, she is the chalice, the womb, topped with doves. We will see more of this in the chapter on the dove and the snake.

PLATE 10 CHAPTER 4

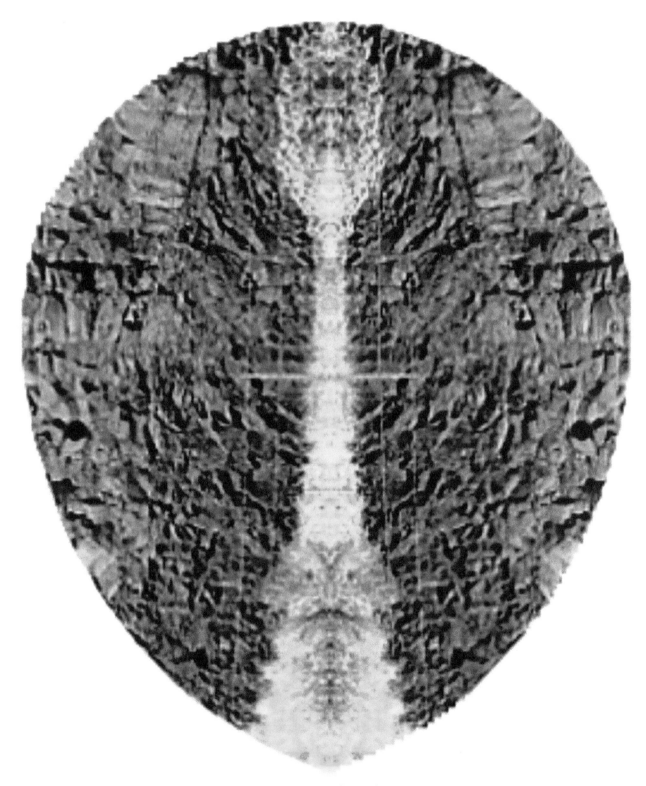

"Arizona mining, with mother's tears"

I cut this picture down to outline her face so we can make it out more clearly. **PLATE 10 CHAPTER 4** was a picture taken of a large mining operation in Southern Arizona. Her tears here are golden. Like the mask, it appears to have the ladder of the *djed* in the middle of her face. I can vaguely make out a scarab pushing up the sun too.

PLATE 11 CHAPTER 4

"New Hampshire mother of the sacrificial stone".

PLATE 11 CHAPTER 4 was taken at New Hampshire's "America's Stonehenge." This place contains a number of megalithic stones, the origin of which is in question. We can clearly see her tears. She appears to have two coiled snakes around her eyes. There is a mask-like feel to this picture too. I can see what appears like the god standing in the center as if we are seeing his backbone, the *djed* in the center of her face. Her face must represent the womb aspect in these mask-like faces. I also see two snakes coming into the picture on either side near the top. Reversed, it looks like the down-under sun that goes down under for rejuvenation.

If I did not see these images of the crying Mother Earth everywhere, I would not be presenting them to you. It shows the need of healing and balance for the divine feminine and masculine in nature and in our human experience once again.

How different we would be acting if we still thought of the Earth as our mother. Some people always have. We treated these people with the same disrespect we have treated mother Earth. This too could be a reason for her tears.

Consciously look for her face in profile and learn the respect the ancients all had at one time for our mother Earth. When we see her crying, we can choose to wake up with her and make better choices for ourselves and our children. Then we too can, once again, live by the law of the feather of Ma'at and learn our rightful place on this Earth.

CHAPTER 5

The Dove and the Snake

I AM AMAZED AT HOW OFTEN I see the dove and the snake together in nature's mirror of symmetry. I see them together in profile as well. Finding them in this way, you see what a phenomenon this is. How interesting that we do not know it is there and have missed this entirely. I hope these pictures can help you learn to look for it and honor it when you see it.

In the Bible, Christ admonishes us to "be ye therefore as cunning as the serpent and as innocent as a dove." Carl Jung describes the serpent and the dove as two halves of the human soul. This means that the dove and the snake are in ourselves as well.

Barbra Walker tells us in her book _The "Woman's Encyclopedia of Myths and Secrets"_ that this saying of Christ's was "no random metaphor." This wisdom went back much further than the time of Jesus. It was, in fact, used as "an invocation of the god and goddess together."

Carl Jung, in his book _"Memories, Dreams, and Reflection's,"_ tells us that together, these two symbols of the dove and snake make a wholeness. It is not surprising then that they are so often seen together in nature. Symmetry somehow makes this visible.

Jung explains that the snake is the masculine principle, and it makes it possible for the dove, which is the feminine principle, to bring her gifts. Her gifts are love, fruitfulness, nourishment, and the promise of a new spring. The snake's gifts are protection and discrimination. When you put them together, they make a powerful whole when they are in balance. When they are out of balance, there is the possibility of stagnation, bareness, and what is better known as a wasteland.

We are living in a time when this balance has been lost. There is the possibility then of making nature into a wasteland. Without this balance within ourselves, it is impossible to claim our rightful power, in a loving and fruitful way. Joseph Campbell, in his book _"The Power of Myth"_, tells us that the dove also represents "the mother conceiving of the spirit." The womb of Mother Nature in symmetry is always accompanied by two doves and two snakes. Together, they bring spirit and matter together.

PLATE 1 CHAPTER 5

"The matrix of Isis the *tjet*".

PLATE 1 CHAPTER 5 from Death Valley, California, placed in symmetry shows the snake and the dove superimposed upon each other. Together, they make a beautiful whole. It reminds me of the ancient Egyptian symbol of the *tjet*. Here, the feminine dove principle stands with the snake in the center like the axis of the world. The axis is also known as the backbone of the world goddess. This is the way it appears in nature. The *tjet* for the Egyptian's "represents the vulva or matrix of Isis," who was considered the Great Mother in Egyptian mythology, according to Barbara Walker's "*The Woman's Dictionary of Symbols and Sacred Objects*".

PLATE 2 CHAPTER 5

"In profile from Northern California".

PLATE 2 CHAPTER 5 shown in profile is a good example of what we will be seeing mirrored in symmetry. In profile, unaltered, the snake is at the top, facing right, and the dove is under it in the rock cliff, also facing right. This is often seen like this with the snake above, the dove below. Amazingly, the dove here almost appears as if it was purposely etched onto the cliff face. This is mother nature's etching.

PLATE 3 CHAPTER 5

"This is plate 2 placed in symmetry."

PLATE 3 CHAPTER 5 placed in symmetry so you can see how symmetry makes it stand out. I enhanced the color to bring out the details. In symmetry, we can see the doves on either side of the chalice/womb. The masculine herm is in the center. This is how opposites come together symmetrically in nature. Two snakes also come together at the top.

Near the bottom in the center, I can see the face of the crone aspect of the feminine. As I have mentioned, she is often considered the womb of the goddess. Her lips are black near the bottom. Like the Celtic Sheela-na-gig image, she is shown here with her mouth superimposed over her vulva.

PLATE 4 CHAPTER 5

"From the same location".

PLATE 4 CHAPTER 5 is another view of the same place, and it looks like a throne of God. The doves and the snakes face inward on either side. I can see a caduceus in this picture too. The axis goes up the center, and the wings at the top of the caduceus go out on either side just below the top, where the snake's curve back into the center. The caduceus is an ancient healing image of opposites coming together that is still used today in the medical profession.

When we reverse this picture, we can see the veiled goddess with her son king at her heart. Her arms are opened to reveal the two doves, which are her totem. All pictures in symmetry are reversible.

PLATE 5 CHAPTER 5

"From Hawaii"

PLATE 5 CHAPTER 5 was taken in Hawaii. The two dove's face inward and upwards in blue violet on either side of the chalice. In this case the two snakes are under them, outlining the chalice as they go into the center on both sides. The goddess's long neck, according to Joseph Campbell, represents the axis mundi. She also appears to be flanked by two geese facing inward on either side. Their beaks are at the top at the level of her chin. Mother Goose was no nursery rhyme. There are many birds that represent the goddess, but it is the doves that represent her womb or chalice.

Reversed, we see the masculine principle, with the snake totem .The chalice now is in the place of his head. In nature, we often see the chalice's as being in her body and his head. This can explain why Sophia is called the wisdom of God and how together, they were co-creators of the world.

From this reversed angle, it seems to be in the shape of an egg. This is what is called the world egg. The world egg is the symbol of the creatures, whose "cosmic egg contained the universe in embryo,"- from Barbara Walker's _The Woman's Encyclopedia of Myths and Secrets_. Often the world egg was associated with primordial surroundings, which, in this picture, is the ocean. It is an image of creation.

PLATE 6 CHAPTER 5

"The doves of Waikiki Beach".

PLATE 6 CHAPTER 5 is a view of Waikiki Beach placed in symmetry. I took this picture from the window of my plane. There is a chalice on the very top with the two doves in the clouds. There are also two doves below this in the center, where there is a boat-like chalice. Being an island, the boat as a chalice is very appropriate. Perhaps this is like the Egyptian sun boat, that gives passage to the sun to be renewed each day. The two snakes seem to be in the green patch just behind the city. In the middle, we see a (V)and reversed, it is an (A). A and V are also symbols of the god and goddess coming together. I see A and V all the time in symmetry. They are usually superimposed over each other like the yin-and-yang sign of nature. Other times, they take on the complete trigram of HAVH.

PLATE 7 CHAPTER 5

"The doves of Northern California".

We see a pyramid shape here. Pyramids are also images of the womb of the goddess, and the two doves in the rocks, face inwards near the top. The two snakes wind themselves from under the doves, going up and over their backs. Perhaps the orange circle at the top is the sun emerging from the pyramid reborn.

Reversed, we see the masculine principle as the bat. The bat is the totem of the dying or death aspect of the god. He is the aspect that is always in the process of dying and being resurrected.

PLATE 8 CHAPTER 5

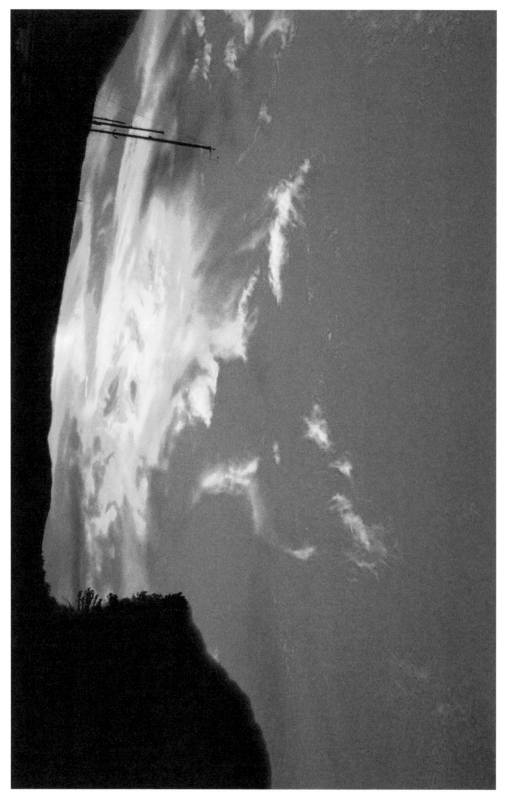

"In Profile"

PLATE 8 CHAPTER 5 shows the divine feminine in profile, with her dove at her neck. She looks like the "woman dressed with the sun"as she faces to the left. This picture was taken at Mount Shasta and shows us once again that the dove is her totem.

PLATE 9 CHAPTER 5

"The dove the snake and the heart".

From the state of Utah, we see the two doves on either side with the heart in the center. The dove has often been considered a symbol of the goddess of love. Here the two snakes are on top of the dove's' heads, just above the beak of the dove.

This also shows a very pronounced caduceus image. The staff goes up the center, with the sun disk on top, just inside the top of the heart. The wings of the caduceus go out on either side of the heart. Nature, when in balance like this, is a very healing force.

PLATE 10 CHAPTER 5

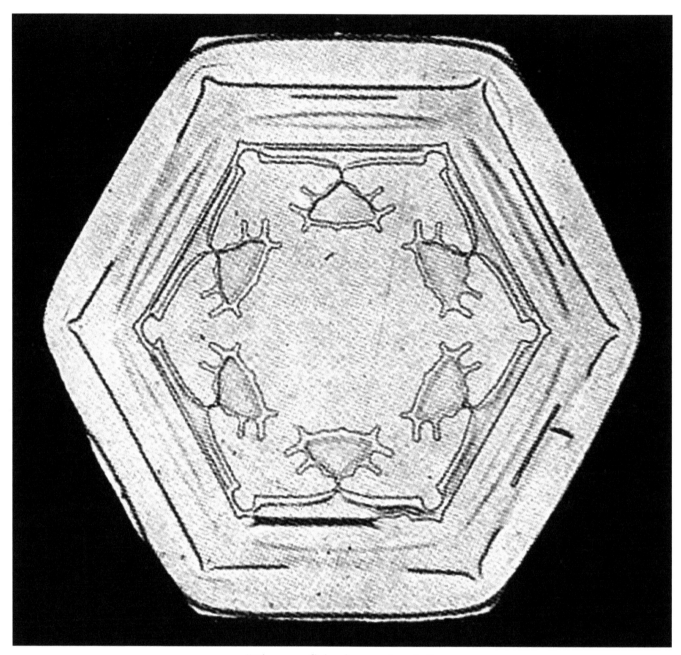

"The snowflake dove and snake".

I love finding these archetypal images in something as small as a snowflake. **PLATE 10 CHAPTER 5** was taken by William Bentley and appears in his book *"Snow Crystals"*, from Dover Press Publications. We can see clearly the doves at each of the six corners of this snowflake all facing outward from the center. The snakes are on top of their wings, going up to the dove's' heads. Together, they are united in something smaller than the eye can see without a microscope.

PLATE 11 CHAPTER 5

"Her Dove and snake mask in profile"

On this cliff by the sea, I found the dove goddess in profile. To see her, you need to turn the picture on its side so that the sky is on the right side. She appears to be wearing a mask, and the dove and the snake are united in her face mask. On the top of her head, we see the dove, and the snake is below, in the darker gray section by her eye. I often see the goddess in symmetry with snakes around her eyes. Perhaps this is the balance with the wisdom of the snake. Her mouth is near the bottom on the right. I can see tears coming out of her eye too.

Edward Edinger, in his book "_The Bible and the Psyche_", also talks about the symbolism of the dove. He writes about a Jewish legend where Moses wanted to war with the descendants of Lot. "God forbade this, saying that the two nations must be spared because two doves were to spring from them." These two doves were likened to the Moabitess Ruth, and the Ammoritess Naamah, wife of Solomon.

Edinger says that one version of this legend has God saying that he "lost something valuable among them." Edinger writes that "we can understand the lost value to be the dove aspect of the feminine principle." This was one of the losses brought about by the patriarchal age.

Like Ruth, the lost feminine principle has had to sojourn on her own. This too was the plight of the Shulamite in the "Song of Solomon". Maybe it is time for the doves to be found again. Maybe the divine masculine needs to come together with the divine feminine in wholeness within and without. Maybe we are to be a part of this coming together and help the divine feminine birth this new beginning.

In talking about the dove symbolism, Edinger says that Sophia wisdom of God, Aphrodite, and the Holy Spirit share the same symbolism with the dove. It would be interesting if the Holy Spirit aspect of the trinity were feminine. I am sure there would be a lot of opposition to that idea.

Carl Jung, in a vision, saw and related to a dove girl, who he later identified as his soul or anima. This was what enabled him to discover what he defined as the "collective unconscious," which was one of his major accomplishments. The dove brings a wealth of enlightenment. We just have to find it sojourning in the foreign land of our unconscious minds.

In **PLATE 11 CHAPTER 5**, the dove appeared to me as a matronly, wise woman who is veiled. Barbara Walker tells us two tales about the veiled goddess. There is an ancient temple in Sais with the inscription "No man has ever lifted the veil that covers me."

The white goddess, Ino Lencalha, was said to have rescued Odysseus from drowning during one of his heroic journeys, by using her divine veil. This would also make her one of the triple goddesses as a bringer of destiny. There is another story a Christian mystic developed who was one of the church fathers. It's about Saint Veronica, "who used her veil to wipe Christ's face as he carried his cross to Calvary." They said that the veil she used "magically took on his true image."

If we look at these stories symbolically rather than literally, we can sense that this aspect of the dove is a sustainer through our hardest trials as we live our true destiny. Her veil can reveal our authentic selves and bring victory out of what feels like a defeat.

I want to know when I come down to the end of my life that I have been in service of something much higher than my ego. We all have a cross to bear, and like the veil of Saint Veronica, when we are suffering because we are true to our destiny, this veil can reveal our authentic selves and bring victory.

The alchemists knew this dove too. One alchemist wrote of the dove Sophia as wisdom incarnate. He wrote, "From the beginning of my birth, I have sought her out and knew not that she was the Mother of all sciences that went before me." "She is an infinite treasure to all men." King Solomon said much the same thing. He knew who she was and sought her out and became the king known for his wisdom.

Even though modern science has progressed, I'm afraid that modern science and technology has yet to seek out the dove in their process. This is dangerous because when this happens, our science becomes imbalanced and can become destructive. We have seen the environmental problems brought about by money and power-based science. I think of pesticides, the proliferation of plastic, the arms race, and nuclear waste.

When the sacred and the wholeness is taken out of our thinking, we are reduced to a control-based and money-making operation. The living balance can only come when the dove is found again. Otherwise, we solve one problem by making another one even worse. Our science needs to be going in a life-affirming direction for the good of all, with the dove and snake in balance.

I think of how science is taught to our children. They are being fragmented by a nineteenth-century debate about creation versus evolution. Both sides are polarized, dogmatic, and materialistic. They show the imbalance with the snake and the dove. If our children accept the side of evolution, they leave out the sacredness and wonder of nature. If they accept what is presented as creationism, they leave their minds and concrete evidence behind. With both, the soul and spirit of life is lost. Many forget in the process that they even have a soul and spirit.

I see hope for the future though. Sophia, the dove mother, is re-emerging again, to help us make this transition from creation versus evolution, to the evolution of creation. If we are able to find the lost dove in this in-between time, truly, we will start to evolve. More people will start to imagine and create ways to clean up and sustain our precious planet. These will be the true heroes of this new age!

We start by focusing on the heart-center that can speak to our whole being. There is a lot of work to do, and much of it will be grass-roots and pioneering. Big egos will have to take a back seat because it's going to take more than just ego's rational thinking, and a for-profit motivation. It will need imagination with heart, and it will definitely need to include Mother Nature's laws and wisdom.

Unfortunately, too much of the government has been bought off. It will take individuals who are working for the good of all to inspire us to move out of our unconscious comfort zone and take positive action. We will have to be present, not passive, and stand behind this new kind of hero, and be open to what we can contribute.

To those with old-school thinking, this new kind of hero might be considered by some to be losers. This is another reason to focus on your center and cut out the noise. If you look back in history, real change doesn't start at the top and trickle down; it pushes its way up from the bottom. Work with your scarab, and don't leave the dove behind.

Make sure you keep your batteries charged. Be encouraged by like-minded people, take time to be in nature, and listen to music that confirms your soul's journey. Make time to turn off your gadgets and attend wisdom. Wisdom is not an app you can download; it is a process and a journey. In this process, our egos are being forged into one that can live their true destiny and give to the world what they uniquely can give. I made a little power song that I can sing to myself like a prayer. It helps me center myself and reminds me why I am pushing forward.

There is a wonderful little story that Laurens Van Der Post tells in his book *"The Heart of the Hunter',* that is full of wisdom from the first peoples of Africa, the Bushman. This is wisdom that comes from watching and listening to nature. In this story, the Bushman tells about the ostrich. He points out that when the ostrich lays its clutch of eggs, it always leaves one egg outside the nest a way's to look at as they sit on their nest. The Bushman laughs a little when he tells the reason for this. Then he tells Laurens that the ostrich is so absent-minded that if it did not have that one egg to look at, it would just get up and walk away, forgetting what it was doing, and none of the eggs would be incubated.

This is so much like us as humans on our inner journey. These eggs represent our potentials and the process of developing what is within ourselves. If we are not mindful of what we are doing, and let the world distract us, we leave our potentials behind. For the alchemist, this is an important part of the work of becoming conscious. Sometimes it takes a while for us to see results. Put that reminder outside your nest, that helps you not to forget what you are here for. Take it one step at a time and attend wisdom.

The ostrich was the creature that the Bushman's hero/god "Mantis", stole fire from. This is another clue to the work. It is like tending a fire, and your job is to not let it go out. Sometimes it can even feel like you are walking on burning ground. The dove is there to help see you through these hard times.

PLATE 12 CHAPTER 5

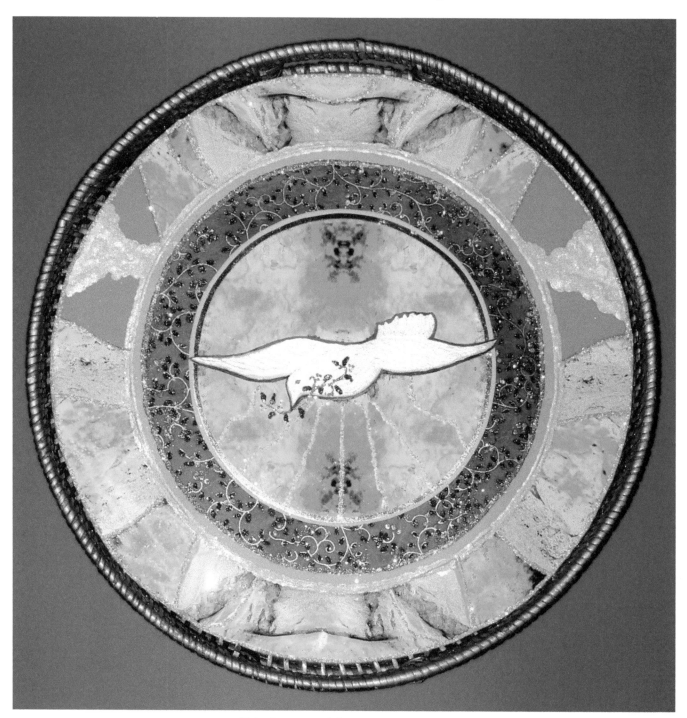

"My dove mandala series over time".

I have made mandalas that have helped mark the progress in my journey. Earlier, I showed the dove mandala that I had made when I was given my beautiful vision. **PLATE 12 CHAPTER 5** was made at a time when it felt like I was walking on some burning ground. The style of this mandala is the target, and it feels like being targeted sometimes when you are in this process. There is a dual nature to this work though. At the same time when, you are feeling targeted, you can also feel comforted and encouraged. In the middle of this mandala is the dove with an olive branch. The blue circle in the middle symbolizes the gold and the waters of life. These are the rewards for persisting in this process. The dove comes through to give the olive branch even as you are going through the fire. This is the fire that burns away the base elements within yourself.

The alchemist admonishes us to despise not the ash because the ash is the final essence of the breakdown of this process. No mistake, this is a time of purging. This is why Carl Jung states in his book *"Psychology and Alchemy"*, that the mind must be in harmony with the work and the work must be above all else." For this reason, the second half of life is best suited for this work. In the second half of life, we are more capable of making this kind of commitment and following through with it. It's also a time when people start to think about what would give them purpose in life beyond simply making a living. Our egos are defined and strong enough at this time to make the necessary sacrifices that put us in service of a higher purpose.

PLATE 13 CHAPTER 5

"The dove has landed" mandala.

PLATE 13 CHAPTER 5 shows that the dove has landed, and it is resting on an open lotus flower. The lotus rises up out of the mud, which is a good description of the process we go through. These are the opposites coming together in a beautiful way. This can represent a rebirth of some kind. The lotus is also a symbol of the womb of the goddess.

Above the dove in the center is the star of the Self, which also shows the opposites coming together as intersecting triangles. At the top, the god wears a headdress with two doves on it. This is a time of the mind being renewed in some way and giving birth to a new life beginning. The two snakes come together under his chin, showing he is the masculine principle of the divine.

There is lightning in two places in this mandala. One is from the head of the god figure, and the other from the hands of Mother Earth, coming out of the upward-pointing triangle in the center. Lightning can represent an awakening, illumination, and transformation that can heal. It is an activating force that is attributed to the divine masculine. Mother Earth's hands helps ground this energy along with the dove. The dove landing on the open lotus is hope that my inner soil is fertile enough to receive this new, energy, and let it do its work. The hands show a willingness to take part in this process and manifest something in the world.

For the Navaho people, the mighty thunderbird brought lightning and thunder. He also brought enlightenment. Lightning can represent a new beginning after a dormant or dark time. This mandala took more time for me to make than most of my mandalas, but when it all came together, it felt like I had done some heavy lifting inwardly.

PLATE 14 CHAPTER 5

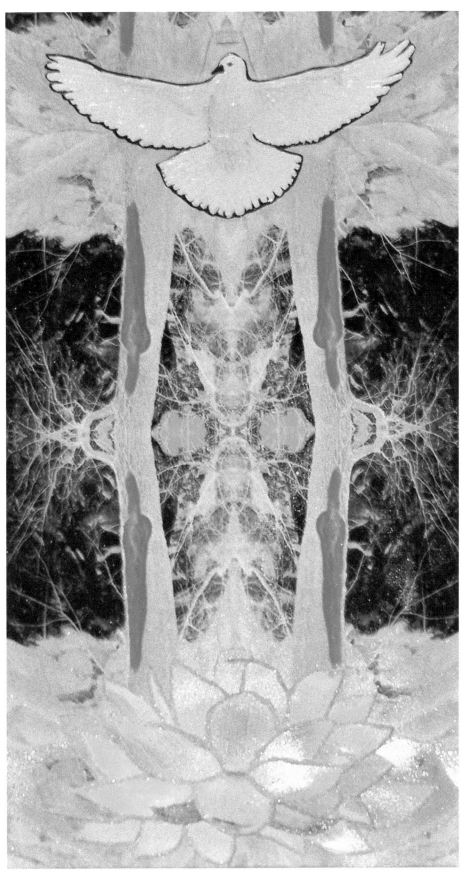

"The ascension"

PLATE 14 CHAPTER 5 shows an ascension of the dove above the open lotus below. It reminds me of the winter solstice, with the birth of the divine masculine. This is the goal of the work when the light comes.

WHAT THE DOVE SHOW'S US COLLECTIVELY

I read a heartfelt article in the *"Smithsonian Magazine"* by William Souder, about an old passenger pigeon (dove) named Martha that died in a drab cage by herself in the Cincinnati Zoological Gardens. He starts his story by telling us how John James Audubon (founder of the Audubon Society) was traveling on horseback in his Kentucky home in the year 1813. He saw a flock of these pigeon doves coming, and he stopped to witness one of the greatest natural spectacles he had ever seen. The birds filled the sky in all directions until the "light of the noonday sun was eclipsed." "All he heard was their buzzing of wings." When he resumed his journey and came to his destination, the pigeons were still flying and "their ranks were undiminished." Their flight continued for days and nights nonstop. Flocks of these birds were estimated at 3.7 billion! This same phenomenon was recorded in Wisconsin, and Ontario, Canada, as well. They were hunted relentlessly, often shot for target practice. They were netted and even burned out of trees. Eventually, they were driven to extinction. Martha was the last remaining bird of her species. Her final years were spent drooping and trembling in a cage by herself. She had to be taken out of the exhibit because people would throw sand and stones at her to make her move. She was very old. These birds could live to be ninety or one hundred years old. Because she could not take the daily abuse of the public, they had to remove her from view.

According to the *Smithsonian*, the curator Helen James said, "Martha represented all that is valuable in nature." What happened to make us so ignorant and disrespectful of the dove and the creatures in nature? This is an indicator of just how severed we have become from the natural world. I think we are learning that what we do to nature, we do to ourselves. We are in great need of the dove that we have lost collectively within ourselves. It is already too late for Martha and her awesome species of pigeon dove's.

Like John Audubon, we need to stop and be present and just observe and listen. We need to record our encounters with the dove within and without. We are learning that progress that contributes to nature's destruction is not progress. Perhaps the "Me Too movement" needs to include our relationship to Mother Nature. Then we will address the need to respect nature, so we do not have to continue the pattern of disrespect, abuse, and neglect of our Mother Earth.

I am hopeful that a new generation of thoughtful and creative young people will hear the mournful call of the dove and demand change. I have heard some of these young people around the world speaking eloquently about having to raise the alarm because we do not have time to ignore these issues any longer. I am encouraged by these young voices.

Carl Jung said, "There is a buried treasure in the soul." We have to find it. That soul is in nature too. How do we know our soul is being tapped? There is an urgency and affect that happens when we tap our soul. Let your outer life be a mirror for your inner life. These connections point to the spirit in matter, which is in everything. This is the spirit that can uplift our hearts if we are listening to the urgent messages of our soul.

There is just one more story I would like to tell you in relation to the dove and the colletive. There was a TV series that some of you may have seen. It was called *"After People."* It was a show about what would happen to life on Earth if people became extinct. One episode showed the relationship between a group of monkeys in a decaying city, whose way of survival included eating dove eggs. There was a catch though. The doves only laid two eggs about six times a year. The question we were left with was, can these monkeys learn to restrain themselves and only eat one of these two eggs, allowing the dove to continue on as a species? If the monkeys were too ignorant, or greedy to restrain themselves, the survival of both species would be lost. By rights, the monkey should be highly invested in maintaining this balance. I am sure the program was making a correlation between the monkeys and our own human condition. All of nature is a balance, and it is a living, breathing balance. When we disrupt that balance, there will be consequences to pay.

In alchemy and in-depth psychology, it was understood that the divine needs our conscious participation in the evolution of consciousness. It is a cooperative effort. We have to show up and do our part. I have a few examples from my experience that may seem insignificant, but in my process, it was the result of tending to my fire.

Often during very difficult times I would wake in the morning with a song in my mind that expressed the feeling in my soul. Once, I woke with thoughts and a feeling of true weariness. This was immediately followed by the song "Balm in Gilead," which makes the wounded whole. You might think that this is just a song I had in my head that I heard all the time. Actually, it had been about forty years since I had heard this song. I had to go on YouTube to get the lyrics. For my soul, this song was a balm and a great encouragement from the dove that morning, in this time in-between sleeping and waking.

I found out that attending to my fire was a great encouragement to Sophia as well, and one morning she acknowledged it. I woke to hear a feminine voice saying, "When I was alone, you comforted me. When I was hungry, you gave me nourishment. When I was thirsty, you gave me drink." It was said in such a way that I got the impression that my mindfulness and attention to my soul work was a real service to the dove in myself. In a real way, our experiences were being mirrored, and it could then become transforming to my whole being. Sophia makes this bridge possible for us if we are willing to attend. This kind of symmetry is necessary for understanding and evolution.

CHAPTER 6

False-face mask time

YOU MAY HAVE SEEN SHAMAN masks of the first peoples of North America that appear like faces that are totally altered. Some show faces pushed totally to one side, distorting the mouth and nose, and others show faces smashed in from the front. This is a mask that reveals rather than hides an experience that the shaman had to endure, before they could claim their rightful power and serve for the good of their people.

The saying "know thyself" applies here. We can try to pass over and even dismiss what is pushed up from our unconscious so we don't have to deal with it, but when it is time to do our work, we must take on this responsibility. At some point, it is not a choice. The false face mask is a symbol and a resulting consequence of this wake-up call.

Shamans are often wounded healers, and before they can help heal others, they must look within their own depths and learn their own strengths, wounds, weaknesses, and limitations. Inflated or deflated ideas about ourselves must be dealt with consciously, and to do this, we must be confronted by the unconscious side of ourselves.

There are two ways in which to experience this confrontation. In both ways, one receives their false face-mask. The first way is claiming too much power and totally underestimating your weaknesses and vulnerabilities. This goes along with the saying "Pride goeth before a fall." I will try to paraphrase a story that was told to me about this form of false facemask and how it is received.

The story begins with a powerful being who thought he was the most powerful being in the world— until one day this powerful being met his creator. He was presumptuous enough to ask the creator, "Who are you?" The creator turned the question around and asked this being, "Who are you?"

Of course, this is a very important question for us all, but if your creator is the one asking this question, it's a real wake-up call. This powerful being told the creator, "I'm the most powerful being in the world, as if it should be obvious." The creator said, "Let's see what you can do."

The being pointed to a mountain nearby and said, "Watch that mountain over there, because I am going to make it move." He concentrated on the mountain until it shook and then moved a whole foot. The creator said, "Indeed, you are a powerful being."

Feeling even more emboldened now, this powerful being, confident he had made his point, said to the creator, "Now let's see what you can do!" The creator told him to turn and look at the mountain again, and before he could completely turn his head, the whole mountain slammed into the side of his face, completely altering it. This was his false face-mask time.

In Jungian psychology, this is called a confrontation with the "activated Self." This is the divine Self, with a capital S. It is not something one is prepared for, it is something one hopefully endures because they were not prepared. Afterward, they are permanently altered. All inflated allusions are shattered, and one is totally humbled.

There is another way to get your false face-mask too. It comes from the opposite direction. It is one of deflation and insecurity or shirking your responsibility. This occurs when one is not willing to claim the power, they have or could potentially have. They would rather project it onto others. It's like the parable of the talents in the Bible, about the person who took the talent they were given and buried it. As a result, it was taken from them. They have the feeling of - I can't do this," or - it is too much of a risk to take. It could be that they just don't want to be bothered.

There is a wonderful true story of an Eskimo shaman and his experience of this false face mask. I was told this story long ago, and I remember it because it spoke to me so strongly. Even though I can't remember his name, I want to thank him for his wisdom freely given. Indeed, he finally claimed his true power and destiny, and I am sure he helped and healed many people on their journeys.

He told how he was having very upsetting dreams of owls pursuing him. He would wake up in a sweat with his heart pounding. Finally, he went to see the shaman of his village to see if he could help him stop having these frightening dreams. The shaman told him that he was being called to be a shaman, and so he would be willing to take him on as his apprentice. This man told him, "No way do I want to become a shaman."

The role of a shaman is not an easy one, because they are often isolated, and misunderstood, so his reaction was understandable. The shaman told this man that if he did not become his apprentice, there was nothing he could do for him. Then he warned him that it would probably get worse for him, not better, until he "answered the call."

It did get worse for him, and he began to be pursued by owls in his waking life as well as in his sleep. It got so bad that he finally went back to the shaman to ask him if there was anything at all he could do for him because it was getting unbearable. Again, the shaman told him there was nothing he could do for him until he agreed to become his apprentice. Again, this man refused. The shaman then warned him that refusing at this point could be a very dangerous decision. It could even be fatal. That proverbial third knock is an ominous one. In a very real way, one is shown their mortality. It is not hard to dismiss the first knock. In fact, we can often question whether it was actually a knock. The second knock is much stronger though and confirms that the first knock was real. It is hard then to just dismiss the second knock, but if you do, it puts you in a different category altogether. You know you are deliberately ignoring a call activated by your higher Self.

The third knock for this man was indeed almost fatal. This can be a fatal experience either physically, psychologically, or spirituality. Part of the man's hesitation was that he felt he had no particular skills or wisdom to offer anyone, so how could he become a shaman? He left the shaman once again without becoming his apprentice.

He was ice fishing one day when someone came up behind him and clubbed him. Then they smashed in his face beyond recognition and left him for dead on the ice. He was found and taken to the shaman. The shaman could see that he could not handle this on his own, so he called two other shamans to come and help him bring this man back from the brink.

It was a long, painful recovery, taking many years of working with these three shamen. Indeed, he had finally become an apprentice. Coming out of recovery, he knew now that he had powerful medicine to share, with a map of his own process to give to others. He was now able to live his true destiny. Sometimes we have to be taken by the scruff of our neck to get our work done in this life.

I saw a picture of him with his false face mask. Most masks conceal the face, but his revealed his permanently altered face. Above his face was a white skull. Perhaps this skull showed how close to death he had come in the process of accepting his calling. It was a powerful mask.

Carl Jung said that "a victory for the Self is a defeat for the ego." The ego likes to think it is in control and can make its own way, and it does until we come up against something much greater than ourselves. This is when we align ourselves with our higher Self and start living our true destiny.

For me, part of the call was to do the hard work of becoming conscious of what my contribution could be for the good of all. I had to learn that what I have to contribute was uniquely mine to share.

PLATE 1 CHAPTER 6

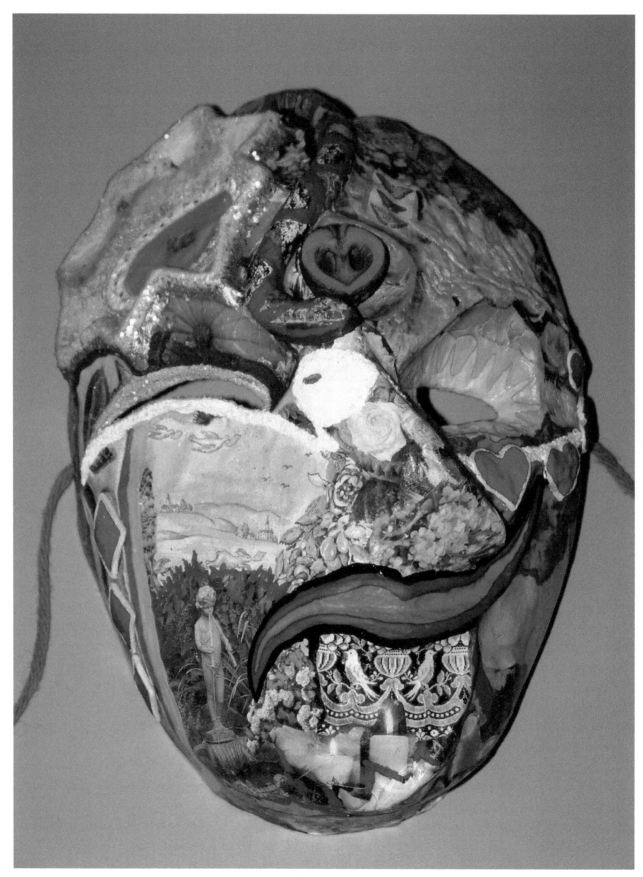

"My false facemask"

PLATE 1 CHAPTER 6 is a picture of my false face mask. It is full of symbols that represent what this experience was for me. When I look at it, it makes me mindful of the process I went through during my own confrontation with the "activated Self" and my false face mask time. Thinking symbolically is important to this process. It helps make meaningful connections that can bring us consciousness.

On the right side (as I wear it), my mask shows what is coming into consciousness. At the top is an eight-cornered star. This represents the Self slamming into my consciousness. Because it has eight corners, it is an influence that is associated with rebirth and the bringing into balance of my conscious mind with my unconscious and higher Self. Since it's on the side of my moon eye, its coming through my unconscious. It is also a sign that there is a destiny I am being called to fulfill.

I was being altered in a permanent way. It was being made clear that my ego was to be in service of something bigger than myself. This is where the work begins. The three red diamonds on this side are the symbol of doing the work in the Tarot. The snake and the dove are being brought together to bring balanced within myself. The snake is the masculine discernment and protection. The dove is the feminine promise of love and fruitfulness. The snake reaches down and touches my third-eye chakra. This is to give me insight into what I need to learn. These are the guardians of the waters of life, that come out of the depths of our soul when we do our work. The nut in the place of the third eye represents awakening, consciousness and wisdom.

Logically, I would have put the sun on the right conscious side and the moon on the left unconscious side. This shows how my life was being turned upside down. The pumpkin above the moon eye shows the gestation that needed to take place as part of working through of my process.

On the lower right side, is the child self and the flute player. I put this at the bottom South section because this is where transformation begins. The South is also the place of childhood, trust and innocence, and the heart.

The flute player is connected to Mother Earth, and like Pan and Kokopelli, he awakens and fertilizes our process. This child self was part of the beginning of bringing balance back into my life so healing could begin. So often we must reconnect to the child and retrieve those parts of ourselves that may have been suppressed, and even shamed, yet they are full of potential that needs to be tapped.

Above him is the rabbit trickster. The trickster tests us to see if we are true and if not, sends us back into our depths to do more work. If the trickster has lied to us, we need to learn to call him out. The rabbit was chosen by Mother moon because of his speed to go down to the earth and encourage everyone by telling them that death is not the end. This experience can feel like a death of some kind. The rabbit came quickly, but like the trickster he was, he told everyone that death was the end. The moon was very angry with the rabbit and gave him what is known as the "hare lip" to show the people that he was not to be trusted.

Mother moon shows us by her waxing and waning that we can go through periods of death and darkness, but the light will return just as the moon becomes full again. Never-the-less, it is the speedy trickster rabbit whose message we get first. We are admonished not to listen to him. This is how I was feeling as I made this mask.

There are birds flying in the sky above the rabbit. Birds often represent the soul in the process of spiritual transformation. Among the birds is the central dove, with her promise of a new spring. On the left side is the sun and the open eye of the conscious mind. Above it, we see the fire that burns off the illusions and the base elements we will have to acknowledge. The fire also leads to a transformation as it goes upward. We see the butterflys representing transformation too.

There are four hearts under this eye that also reach upward on this side. Barbara Walker in her book *Secrets of the Tarot*, tells us that in ancient sacred dramas, the four of hearts represents the declining period "following the consummation and fertilization that brought about the death of the god, who descends into the underworld which marks the down under time of the sun". The four hearts are circling the sun from beneath in my mask. Eventually, this would be followed by a resurrection and a new life cycle.

Most of these symbols were understood after I was analyzing the mask when it was completed. I chose the symbols somewhat instinctively as I thought they would fit, but it wasn't until later that I analyzed it and began to figure it out. It is surprising what the intuition and instincts can show us. This was a period of decline for me. It was an in-between hanging-out time. It also corresponded with the beginning of my third phase of life, which, for a woman, is the time of menopause and the onset of the "wise woman" phase of life.

This can be a difficult transition that takes time and patience. In this phase though, we have the opportunity to re-parent ourselves and give ourselves permission to take some of the opportunities we may have never considered before, and seriously pursue them. The dove in the center of my mask was very encouraging. She is the bridge that brings all these fragments together in a healing way with understanding. She faces with me, this confrontation within myself.

Carl Jung has said in looking back on the ages gone by that the age of the father was Abraham's age of Aries. The age of Christ, the son, was the age of Pisces. Looking forward, he thought the next age', Aquarius, could be the age of the Holy Spirit, the dove. He also thought it would have to be a time for the collective to stop being like children and take on their responsibility for future evolution. l am grateful that the dove is in the center of my mask. So many times, I have heard the mournful but comforting sound of the dove, both within and outside of myself. It has comforted me through these difficult times.

Under the altered mouth, we see candles burning. This is the ego in service of this transforming process. The ego must submit to these trying times and keep the fame going, remembering that life is sacred and that we are here to continue the process of becoming conscious.

Some shamans would not go into their role as healer without their false facemask on. This is an archetypal process in which one is called as a wounded healer to claim their rightful power for the good of all. This mask reminds them that they do not do their work alone by our ego's good management. This is a calling from our higher Self.

In an alchemical book, I saw a picture of the alchemist going into his laboratory. As he goes in, Sophia greets him at the door, the borderline of the work he must do, and she admonishes him not to go in without her. This is the most important thing the alchemist must remember. The dove on my mask reminds me of this.

Joseph Campbell, in his book _The Way of the Animal Powers,_ talks about this experience. He writes about an Eskimo maxim that goes like this: "The only true wisdom lives far from mankind, out in the great loneliness, and it can be reached only through suffering. Privation and suffering alone can open the mind of man to all that is hidden to others."

In this space, one can make contact with the mystery of the soul of the universe. An old Alaskan shaman, Najagneq, tells it this way: "All we know is that it is a gentle voice, like a woman, a voice so fine and gentle that even children cannot become afraid. What it says is, "Be not afraid of the universe."

I heard this woman's gentle voice during my difficult period too. She had a very real question for me. She asked me how far I wanted to go with this process. I had to think for a moment before I answered her because I knew my answer was important. I told her that I did not know what I was capable of nor how much I could handle. Since She knew me better than I knew myself, I would let her decide how far to take me. I was willing to follow. This was my answer to the dove during my false -face mask experience. Because of her gentle voice, I knew I did not need to fear. This was the way I went into the laboratory of my soul work, not leaving Sophia behind.

CHAPTER 7

Spider Woman "Weaver of Life"

"If you bring forth what is within you, what you bring forth will save you. If you do not bring forth what is within you, what you do not bring forth will destroy you". —The <u>Gospel of Thomas</u>

THE ANCIENTS OF MOST CULTURES had an archetype known as the weaver of life. A few of her names were Spider Woman and Thinking Woman. In Celtic tradition, she is known as Brighid. To the Greeks she was Athene. She was revered as the co-creator in the weaving of our lives. There are many mythic stories and adventures written about Spider Woman, as weaver of life. This chapter will tell you my story about Spider Woman and her influence in my life.

First, I want to make something clear that has been twisted by modern logic. Myths and mythic stories are not stories that are untrue; they are stories that describe truths. These truths are only understood when they are lived, and so when they are presented as a story, we can then find ourselves in these stories as we live and learn from them. They then become part of our lives as wisdom stories for us.

I am surprised by how religious training often teaches spiritual understanding as little more than historical realities and facts. When we do this, the symbols and metaphors that make these stories meaningful can be lost. These stories are universal and timeless. Wisdom is not a brand that belongs to one culture. No one culture has a monopoly on wisdom. When we think of wisdom as if ours is the only true wisdom, it is easy to disregard the wealth of wisdom from other cultures and other ages gone by. To other people, this attitude comes across as arrogance, and it limits what we ourselves can learn. If we can let down our self-imposed guard, we can begin to learn this universal wisdom.

The divine feminine likes to teach with the use of symbols and stories, so thinking symbolically, as I have said, is an important part of the process of growing and evolving. We can learn to look for the experiences and the symbols that can make us conscious, or we can blindly become unconscious victims of the patterns and circumstances we have no understanding of. We can evolve in a conscious manner if we let Spider Woman lead us through our experiences with stories, symbols, and our dreams. This is how we find what we need to learn.

She teaches us at the appropriate time when we are ready to learn. When this happens, they become like medicine or healing stories. To go in this direction, we have to be willing to attend wisdom. This becomes our work, and in the process, we become our true authentic selves with experience under our belts, not just belief systems handed down or forced upon us. We can then see a bigger picture, not a rigid dogma we must try to fit into. This is the wisdom that brings us home to ourselves and gives us meaning.

One of Carl Jung's patients came to him on the brink of a psychological breakdown. He did something amazing for this patient. Every time she came to a session, he told her as many stories as he could. At one session, his patient asked him why he was spending all these sessions just telling stories. Instead, why was he not dealing with her problem? He told her that these stories would be what would help her make it through her ordeal in the end.

Stories are like containers, and the stories he was telling her helped contain her when she finally did have a breakdown. When she came out of her episode, she told Jung that indeed, it was the stories he had told her that helped pull her through. This was the genius of Carl Jung. Many shamans work with people in this same way as well. First, they find the image or symbol of the problem and then the story for the person they are trying to help heal, and they go from there. Often psychiatrists today, prescribe drugs, and send their patients on their way. This does not heal; it only covers up their problem.

Spider Woman brings us understanding from the heart as well as the head. For this reason, she has been called the Mother of the Enlightened Ones. It usually takes time to recognize her role in our lives. The ancients gave a reason for this. They called it glamour or illusion. This is a defense mechanism our egos use to prevent us from seeing what we do not want to see or deal with. This is a clue, that our ego's need to be attending wisdom if we are to make any progress in our work.

We need Spider Woman collectively too as we make this chaotic transition into a new age. She has been called the "mistress of perceptive reality, and the midwife that helps us give birth to a greater reality," from Barbara Walker's book "*The Woman's Encyclopedia of Myths and Secrets*".

I remember the first big dream I had when Spider Woman was trying to make a breakthrough into my consciousness. I was about thirty-one, and I was just beginning to seriously look at and study my dreams and my symbolic life. She knew I was sincerely ready to begin my journey with her and start to gather her medicine for my life.

In this powerful dream, I was walking up the street of my childhood home. I was walking beside our neighborhood drug-store, called "Webb's Drugs." As I looked back on this symbolically, this could be interpreted as Spider Woman's medicine. Across the street from Webb's Drugs was a community church that was known for holding many social events, both secular and religious. The scene in the dream changed, and I found myself in the basement of this church.

There were long lines of people waiting to receive a cloak. This was a special cloak that had woven into the design the fate of the person who would wear it. The designs were all unique and different, and everyone was curious to see what the outward design of their cloak would look like. Even after receiving their personalized cloak however, they were unaware of what it meant. Unquestioningly these people waited their turn in line.

In the dream, I stood looking at the proceedings and wondered if I was supposed to get in line with them. I was questioning the process, but at the same time, I was curious about the design that would be on my cloak.

As I stood there hesitating, a Wise Woman walked up to me. She seemed to be the only one there who understood what was going on. She told me that I did not need to get in the line where I would have a cloak assigned to me. She told me I could learn to make my own design for my cloak, and she would help me do this. She explained to me that many people would rather not have to take on the responsibility of becoming conscious and take part in creating their own destiny. Those people would simply receive the fate assigned to them. She said that if some of these people who were passively accepting their cloaks knew what their fate would be, they would be horrified. By going on my own, with her help, I had the opportunity to learn, imagine, and help weave my own design for my true destiny. We started to leave the church together, and at this point, "I woke up".

I say "woke up" because this was one of those important dreams of my life. Big dreams don't come very often, but when they do, it's important to "wake up", get the message, and learn what it's about. This dream was a gift from Spider Woman, full of clues from my higher Self to help me evolve into the person I could potentially become. I want to know for myself when I come to the end of my life that I fulfilled what I had come here to do and did my best.

This is the job of the alchemist, who must take the base material of their lifes and turn it into gold. I was leaving the basement of this church. The basement of the church symbolically represented a place of spiritual unconsciousness, which is where many people would rather be. Becoming conscious requires us to be willing to learn to recognize the opposites in ourselves and balance the wild and unacceptable parts of ourselves as well as the conscious, structured ego parts of ourselves. We must claim the weak and darker parts of ourselves, not just our strengths. When we learn to find the symbols that relate to us, then we know Spider Woman is helping us. We can then begin to weave our conscious mind and our unconscious mind together to make a new whole.

We need to use our imaginations and pay attention to the signs put before us as we seek a new direction. Life is about authentic experiences that are motivated by our inner self. We need to get out of the line of unconscious acceptance of the norm and the expected if we want to create a true destiny. We need to be the ancestors for our children who allow them to get the experiences they need to get their chance of becoming co-creators of their lives. We can only do this by becoming conscious.

We are getting warnings from teachers, doctors, and scientists that we are going in a direction that is not getting our children's needs met and that in fact, it could be harmful to them. We need to wake up and start imagining new ways to address these issues. These are grassroots issues, and we can't wait for the government to address these after the fact. We need to hold their feet to the fire and work with them for change. The world needs more creative and innovative individuals who know themselves and what they have to contribute to the world.

Recently I heard some things in the news that shocked me to my core. One was a story of an eight-year-old girl who was taking her dog for a walk in her own neighborhood. A policeman stopped her and took her home and asked her mother why her daughter was unattended. Her mother could not believe that her daughter could not even walk her dog without being picked up by the police. It was as if it was too dangerous for her and therefore unacceptable. How sad if this is the case! We hear all the time about children of color who can't even walk down the streets of their own neighborhoods without danger, even from the police. Again, I wonder, where do these children play? Play is a childs way of learning. Have we forgotten this?

The next day, I read an article in the newspaper where a doctor was reporting that he was actually prescribing more unsupervised play for some of his child patients. He said children need to use their imaginations, make their own rules, and have their own experiences if they are to be healthy. Why do we have to be told this by a doctor? The only things getting good exercise is our childrens thumbs when they are using their phones and devices. This does not give them authentic experience, it gives them virtual reality. We are starting to hear the voices of our younger generation, and they are feeling cheated. At what point do we begin to wake up and work with them and make sure they start getting their needs met?

In my process of working on myself, I use mandalas as part of my work. I have done mandala projects with children as well, and it has been very meaningful for them. Mandalas allow children to go into their own space and put out into the world something that authentically represented themselves in that moment. One girl mentioned that making her mandala was the most fun project she had ever done.

One boy who was a foster child just about to be moved to another set of foster parents made his mandala as the last project he had done before he had to go to a new home and school. He worked so hard on this mandala, and it was so important for him to be able to finish it so he could hang it in his new room, where ever that would be. His mandala showed that he was visibly scared of what he was about to face, but this was his attempt at making order out of the chaos in his life. What tools are we giving to our children to help them in their process? Like the opportunities to play, some of this is just plain common sense that has somehow been lost.

PLATE 1 CHAPTER 7

"My Spider Woman Mandala".

PLATE 1 CHAPTER 7 shows my process of working on myself with Spider Woman as I was going through my menopause transition into the "wise woman" phase of my life. I made this mandala in a meditative and prayerful manner so I could learn to work with her and my own unconscious. I start by mindfully gathering materials and symbols, and then I put them together like a meditation. With mandala making, there is much more at work than the ego agenda in fact, it is best to pull yourself out of ego mode when preparing for this project. To begin with, you put yourself in the position of being a witness of yourself where you can be as open about what you learn as possible.

This is my Spider Woman/Wise Woman mandala. In the center, we see in fact, what looks like a spiderweb. This was not deliberate on my part. It was only when I had studied it later that I found this symbol. In a mandala, a spider in her web in the center of a mandala is thought of as an incarnation of the goddess as the spinner of life. Psychologically, in a young person, it could indicate a mother complex. In the "wise woman" phase of life however, it can be a very positive symbol of transformation. This was my prayer as I made this mandala. The seven blue butterflies around the center are a good indicator that a transformation is taking place. There are seven bees too. Bees, from an alchemical standpoint, are the creatures that literally make the gold. They do the work. This is what I wanted to do with myself.

The style of my mandala is a target style. With this style there is the experience of feeling like I am in the eye and work is being done or needs to be done on me. This mandala even looks like an eye. There is a circle of brown dirt around the outside of this mandala. This is dirt that I collected in a sacred manner along the Virgin River in Utah. This brings in the element of earth for grounding this experience. Psychologically, this would also pertain to the sensation function, which is my weakest function. This would be even more reason to have grounding for my experience. It also tells me that I am still unconscious of the process at this point and that this is not my ego agenda. It makes it like the virgin's process, with my ego in a receptive hands-off meditative mode. In this situation, this allows the divine to enter and help in the work. My ego will not block the way. I am open to something higher.

I placed this mandala in a basket weave for framing the weaving of my life in this moment. This is also another good symbol of Spider Woman. There was also the symbolic influence of Sophia, Mother Wisdom, with her house built of seven pillars. These pillars are in-between each petal. Each petal shows the alchemical work of turning base metal into gold.

A turquoise circle surrounds both the blossom and the very center. Turquoise has always been symbolic of the divine feminine for me. There are small red dots in the blossom petals. This would represent for me the sacrifice of my ego agenda in the process of becoming conscious. I want to be an ego in service of a higher purpose. The turquoise blossom in the center represents the divine feminine aspect of the self.

Carl Jung considered mandala work to be an attempt by the psyche to become whole and conscious. Even if you don't understand it when you make it, there is at least the attempt at making order out of a chaotic fragmented situation in an uncertain transformational time.

I use Susanne F. Fincher's book - *Creating Mandalas* to help me interpret my mandalas. It is a wonderful reference for understanding and interpreting your mandalas after you make them. This is soul work, and it connects us to our center. This is work that helps in the birthing process of our journey in a spiritual way. Mandalas can assist in transitioning into a new direction in life. It is a way for our egos to participate actively without controlling or forcing its own agenda. It is an ego attending wisdom and working with your higher Self.

Carl Jung said that psychological maturity means "The responsible living and fulfilling of the divine will in us." This is attending wisdom.

CHAPTER 8

Spider Woman on the Axis Mundi

Let's see Spider Woman in the hidden third of symmetry. The ancients were right – she is there! In Arizona, at the Canyon De Chelly National Monument, there is a natural megalithic rock formation that the first peoples of the American Southwest honored and named "Spider Rock". This is Spider Woman's rock, and it towers high above the canyon floor, straight and tall as if it marks the very center axis of the world.

PLATE 1 CHAPTER 8

"Spider Woman's Rock".

PLATE 1 CHAPTER 8 is the symbolic connection that goes from the deep center of the earth clear up into the cosmos. At the top of this rock, there is what appears to be an image of a spider seated on the top. The spider of course, is Spider Woman's totem. There is such a beautiful view from this spot, and I just stood here for some time, imagining the wise ones and shamans of the past who, in their imaginations, used this towering megalithic stone as an axis in their trance to make the meditative journey up to the upper world or down into the depths to bring wisdom and healing back to their people.

As I was on the way back to my car, a Navaho man approached me and sold me a replica of a petroglyph that he said depicted the celestial landscape of this place. I am glad I bought it because it helped me remember and ground this experience. Once again it was something concrete in real time that would remind me of this sacred place with Spider Woman.

PLATE 2 CHAPTER 8

"Kokopelli and the petroglyph of the Axis Mundi".

PLATE 2 CHAPTER 8 represents this place and shows the axis with the image of Kokopelli, the fertilizing masculine principle climbing up the ladder that goes into the heavens. This is like a "Tree of life", or the Ankh image that connects us to life and the universe.

Under Kokopelli's feet, we see the scorpion, which could possibly represent the astrological sign of Scorpio, which also represents the home of the galactic center. The month of Scorpio marked the time of the declining year and the death of the old sun. This dark void in Scorpio was considered the womb of the galaxy, taking in the old sun that was weak and spent at the end of October and the beginning of November. It is also known as the days of the dead, and then finally giving birth to the new sun on the winter solstice.

The moon above him is the closest connection we have to the heavens and our first step to the stars. Many older cultures had lunar calendars at one time, and some still do. The moon and stars were visible together, and the ancients studied them and even navigated and traveled by them. It reminds me that these people were much more connected to the heavens than we are today. City lights have replaced the wonder and rhythm of the heavens for us.

PLATE 3 CHAPTER 8

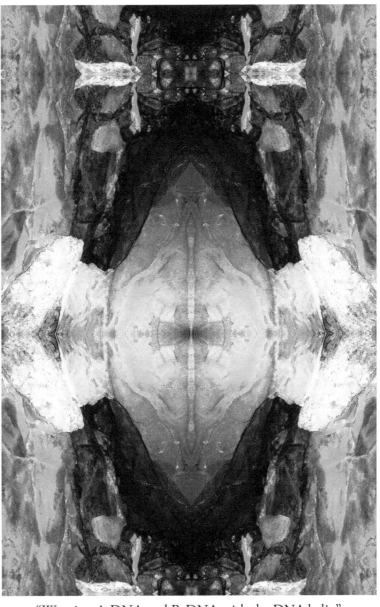

"Weaving A-DNA and B-DNA with the DNA helix".

PLATE 3 CHAPTER 8 of Spider Woman was from a cave picture placed in symmetry. Spider Woman connects us to the underworld as well as the heavens, and she can take us down into our depths to retrieve what may have been lost, neglected, or stolen within our lives.

Like her megalithic rock, the spider in this image sits on the very top, where her face would be. Her face appears to be in the starry heavens. The axis pole goes down through her center. She could also be a chariot, with wheels on either side of her. We are all charioteers on this Mother Earth, and she carries us all to our fate or to our destiny, depending on which we choose.

I see two bright red-orange threads with which she weaves our lives together, like the strands of DNA we are given at birth. If you look at her head closely, you can see the outline of the A-DNA and B-DNA patterns that run through everything. These patterns can be seen in plate 13 of this chapter. They are superimposed over one another. This is the weft and warp of the weaving of our lives.

PLATE 4 CHAPTER 8

"She appears to me in the woods ."

PLATE 4 CHAPTER 8 was a gift from Spider Woman. As I was becoming conscious of her presence, I came across her in the woods. There she was, right in front of me. This picture has not been altered, so we have to look at this image in profile to see the significance of it. Spider Woman is facing left, and she appears to be pregnant and in the process of weaving life within herself. We can only see her torso; her face is not visible. This is because she is weaving the future, which cannot be seen. The tree in the background goes through her like the World Axis. This picture confirmed to me that the center of the world is everywhere. We just need to recognize and honor it. This was a sacred moment for me.

PLATE 5 CHAPTER 8

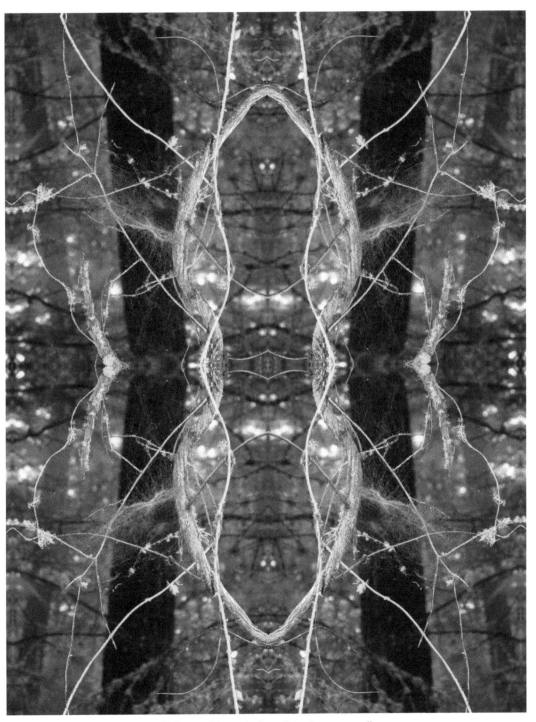

"This is Plate 4 placed in Symmetry".

When **PLATE 5 CHAPTER 8** was placed in symmetry, we can see her totem the spider, right in the center of her body. The spider appears to be made of two very strong cords that look like bows ready to be pulled and the arrow of life released into the world. There is a glow about her that lets us know she is also related to the sun just as the earth is related to the sun.

PLATE 6 CHAPTER 8

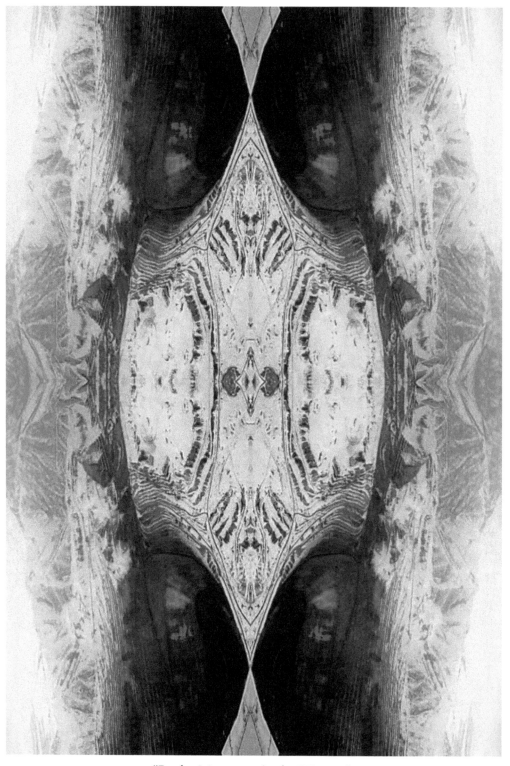

"Rocky Mountain Spider Woman".

PLATE 6 CHAPTER 8 of Spider Woman was taken as I was flying over the Rocky Mountains of Utah. I took the picture from my airplane window on my way to Salt Lake City. There was a mining operation going on below that exposed the bare earth where they had been mining. It was spring-time, so there was still a blanket of snow on the ground.

When I put this picture into symmetry, there she was, standing straight and tall over the Rocky Mountains. Here again, her face is not visible. I have seen pictures of the divine feminine often without a distinct face. Sometimes she is veiled or masked, and sometimes only her torso is seen. The ancients made images of the goddess with blank, or capped faces. It wasn't until later in history that they started to make images of the goddesses as beautiful women.

My first impression when I saw this picture in symmetry was how beautiful her white garment of snow was. Unfortunately, the mining operation had exposed her breasts and thighs. I was reminded of the American Indian stories of "White Buffalo Woman," who visited their people to give them her wisdom for living in a sacred manner.

The story goes that two hunters saw her walking towards them in a beautiful white gown. One of the hunters could see she was a sacred being, but the other lusted after her. It was a reminder of how much we need her wisdom today if we are to live once again in a sacred manner. This mining operation shows the marks of the hunter who had lusted after her.

When we look at this picture horizontally, we can see the pyramids and chalice/womb at the top. The double doves and double snakes are accompanying this image. Near the top, coming into the center but just off to the sides, I see the beaks and necks of two geese. Perhaps she is related to Mother Goose also. Mother Goose is the feminine aspect who laid the golden egg, also thought of as the sun. There appear to be pyramids of the sun here on either side of the center at the top.

PLATE 7 CHAPTER 8

"By the Sea."

I found **PLATE 7 CHAPTER 8** of Spider Woman in front of a small cave by the sea on the Oregon Coast. In symmetry, there is no mistaking the spider in the center. It appears as if she is in the alchemical process of turning base material into gold. This is what is known by the alchemists as the "great work." She is indeed one who assists us in this process of becoming conscious and making gold from the base material in our life.

This picture makes a cross in the center. This is the cross we as humans must bear in the process of becoming whole. Often-times it is our very own DNA that is woven into our lives that poses our greatest challenges. Without it though, we cannot find the gold hidden there in what the alchemist called the "prima materia" of our lives. How would we learn if there were no challenges for us to face?

PLATE 8 CHAPTER 8

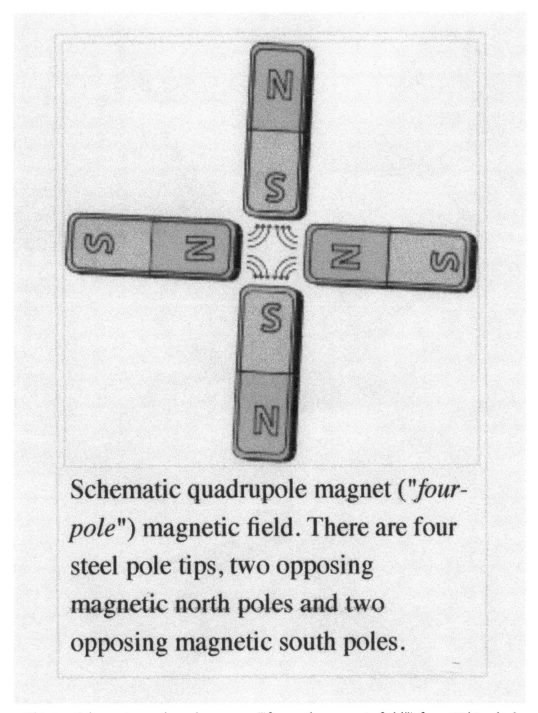

Schematic quadrupole magnet ("*four-pole*") magnetic field. There are four steel pole tips, two opposing magnetic north poles and two opposing magnetic south poles.

This is a Schematic quadrupole magnet ("four-pole magnetic field") from Wikipedia.*

Wikipedia shows **PLATE 8 CHAPTER 8** of what is called a Schematic quadrupole magnet with two opposing magnetic north poles, and two opposing magnetic south poles. It looks like a simple cross with an open center that connects all sides. I found what looks like an example of the description of this in a cave picture I put in symmetry.

The graphics are more elaborate in Spider Woman's pictures than the simple diagram of a magnet in the shape of a cross given by Wikipedia's diagram. When you look at them closely though, they are very similar. It is interesting that symmetry can show us these images that describe what science has tried to describe in a much more rudimentary way.

* Image by ©Wikipedia

PLATE 9 CHAPTER 8

"Spider Woman's rendition of the Schematic quadrupole magnet".

In my imagination, **PLATE 9 CHAPTER 8** is a wonderful example of the process of how Earth's magnetic field works. Wikipedia gives a description of the Meridional magnetic field as the one that runs north -to -south. They talk about a process called the omega -effect, where the solar plasma causes the meridional magnet field to stretch into an azimuthal magnetic field, which is it's opposite. Although I am not coming at this from a scientific standpoint, I can see this stretching of the solar plasma going on here. This is a picture taken in a cave, placed in symmetry. I get some amazing pictures in caves after I place them in symmetry.

PLATE 10 CHAPTER 8

"Spider Woman weaves the opposites together".

PLATE 10 CHAPTER 8 is a great example of the divine feminine as Spider Woman with the feminine A-DNA seen from this direction, and the masculine B-DNA seen from the opposite direction. The masculine takes on the inward curving H like we see on ancient sun disks or like in the center of the Mayan stone calendar. Again, A-DNA and B-DNA are superimposed over each other. This is how Spider Woman does her weaving. It is also like a magnetic attraction happening. As they say, opposites attract.

PLATE 11 CHAPTER 8

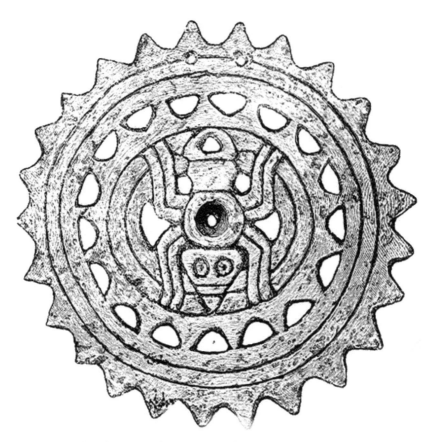

"Authentic Indian design of Spider Woman".*

PLATE 11 CHAPTER 8 is an ancient American Eastern Woodlands design of Spider Woman with the sun. I found this image in the book *"Authentic Indian Designs"*, edited by Maria Naylor and published by Dover Press. This prehistoric design shows an image of Spider Woman overlaid against a sun disk. It has the appearance of Spider Woman being in the eye of the sun. This would go along with the idea of the sun and Spider Woman as being related to insight and consciousness. This can be why Spider Woman is also called Thinking Woman.

---

* Image by ©Dover Press. Image edited by Maria Naylor (permission is granted)

PLATE 12 CHAPTER 8

"Spider Woman as earths magnetic field".

PLATE 12 CHAPTER 8 gives a close rendition of what the Earth's magnetic field looks like from space. In my Google search, I found many artists' renditions of this phenomenon. This magnetic field looks very much like a spider. This is the magnetic field that protects us from harmful sun storms that would otherwise break into our atmosphere. I can see many different creatures in this picture also, which tells me she protects all her creatures.

When I think of this psychologically, I realize why it is that Spider Woman needs to help us on our journey to becoming conscious. With her help, we are guided and protected.

PLATE 13 CHAPTER 8

A-DNA Female

B-DNA Male

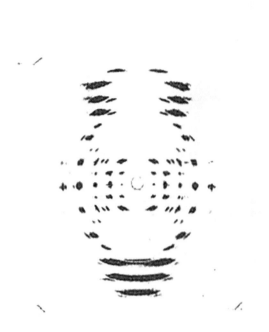

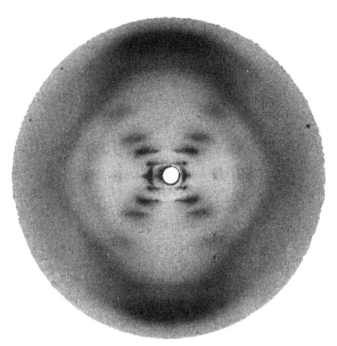

"A-DNA and B-DNA as the threads of Spider Woman]

PLATE 13 CHAPTER 8 shows the first photos ever taken of (A and B DNA) by Rosalind Franklin in the early 1950's. They were first shown by Maurice Wilkins in the 1952 Nobel lecture at the Nobel Prize Foundation. Rosalind Franklin died of X-ray poisoning because of her extensive research using X-ray exposure to capture these images. Her work was invaluable in the discovery of DNA.

Looking at these two pictures, we can see the same patterns in the center of so many of my pictures in symmetry. The A-DNA is the feminine principle and B-DNA is the masculine principle. I will see them often superimposed over each other vertically and horizontally.

A good example of this was plate 10 of this chapter. Plate 12 shows a good example of A-DNA. In plate 3, we can see them superimposed over each other in Spider Woman's face. Spider Woman is the archetype who in fact, weaves these strands together. Plate 4 of Chapter 2 also shows us a good example of B-DNA, the masculine principle. It amazes me that DNA patterns run through everything we look at, and in symmetry, we can actually see them.

I hope with all the research in physics and biology today, we are using these patterns of life, in a good way, for the good of all. I also hope they are going to let their knowledge become wisdom for us all. If this wisdom is not respected world wide, we will most likely use this understanding to compete with, and even to war on others. It would certainly bring about destruction if we do not honor this as sacred.

CHAPTER 9

Scarab Work Is a Symbolic Life That Transforms

PREPARING FOR A GRADE SCHOOL mask-making art project, I had the idea of enlarging pictures of the backs of scarab-like bugs, because the symmetry of their backs made them appear like faces. The children could enjoy coloring and embellishing them to make creative masks. I spent most of this particular afternoon at the copy machine enlarging these scarab bugs to the appropriate size for the children's faces. When I got home, I was alone in the house because my husband was spending the weekend with his gold-prospecting buddies. As one who appreciates symbolism and Jungian psychology, I look back on this weekend's experience and think to myself that my animus, (my masculine unconscious counterpart) to my feminine ego was also gold prospecting in my own psyche. My animus was helping the scarab do its work to dig through the prima materia of my life to push up the sun of consciousness.

Rather than eating at the table alone, I decided to eat dinner in front of the TV. After dinner, I fell asleep on the couch. When I woke up, there was a movie in progress. It was a World War ll movie about the covert activities that were taking place to sabotage the Nazi's in Germany. The movie was so surreal that it felt like I was in a dream and this dream had a message for me. I can usually sense when there is a message for me by the amount of affect it stirs up.

I was glued to the TV as I watched this very little man carrying a large briefcase down a city street with large imposing government office buildings lining it. It appeared to be after normal business hours because there were few people on the street. When this little man got to the corner, he sat on a bench and pretended to read a newspaper. He was waiting for the right moment to start his work. Finally, he opened his briefcase and took out a huge scarab-like bug.

Right there, my attention level went from waking up to wide awake. The synchronicity of this imagery was impossible for me to ignore. I had just spent the entire afternoon enlarging scarab-like bugs for my grade school classes (the little people).

The scarab this little man pulled out of his briefcase was wearing three two-gun holsters strapped around its body. He placed the scarab on the side of the building next to him and watched it climb up to an open window. This window led into a hallway lined with the offices of high-ranking Nazi officers. The scarab waited as three women who appeared to be prostitutes left one of the offices. The Major General himself smugly opened the office door for them as they left and closed the door behind them.

This must have been a signal because now the scarab climbed in and walked up to the major general's door and knocked. The scarab stood poised with two of his guns ready to shoot. When the officer opened the door, the scarab started shooting. The officer had just enough time to pull his gun and shoot off one shot at the scarab before the officer fell dead. His one shot ricocheted off the wall and grazed the scarab, which then hobbled to the window and crawled back down to the little man waiting below. The little man could see the scarab had been shot and told the scarab not to worry, he would fix it back up again, good as new. He then placed the scarab back in his briefcase and quickly left to go back down into his underground hiding place. At this point, it felt like this hiding place was in the underground of my own psyche. It was hard for me to continue watching the rest of the movie. I almost didn't want to see it because the little man found out that his underground hiding place had been compromised, and he had to find another place from which to do his work. Being tired, I fell asleep again, and when I awoke, the movie was over. This movie had disturbed me enough though, to make me finally write it down in my journal before I went to bed.

Synchronicities are events of meaningful coincidence when your inner and outer lives come together and mirror each other in a significant way. These experiences are symmetrical, and they come together to shed light on and confirm something you are becoming aware of. If you are being attentive, it is a confirmation that you are on your path, doing your work. Often there is affect involved, making it even more of a personal and emotional message. Sometimes it can be so strong that it feels like another part of yourself is watching you and they know you better than you do.

The purpose of the scarab's message is to lead us to a higher level of self-understanding. It becomes a doorway to a dimension you would normally not reference for. If you don't go in this doorway, the clues that are given are lost as easily as the details of a fleeting dream.

The keys to this doorway are the symbols that are brought up for you to see and understand. This is why inner work requires a symbolic life. Our unconscious and the divine feminine speaks to us in images, so it is important for our psychological and spiritual development to learn these symbols and work with them.

Even if it takes years to understand these symbols, writing them down and pondering them helps the scarab do its work. If you ignore these experiences, you stunt your growth and find yourself in a cycle of reoccurring self-sabotage and denial that prevents you from moving forward. If we open ourselves to these messages, they can take us on the path of evolution and understanding. Life then becomes meaningful and purposeful on a higher level.

Carl Jung thought these chance events to be so important, he considered it our responsibility as evolving individuals to pay close attention, and own what needs to be owned, and learn how to understand what these symbols mean in our lives. As long as you are in (the eye) of this work, you need to pay attention and show up for the lessons they give, even if it makes you feel uncomfortable. Now your higher Self knows you are willing and ready to learn, and take responsibility for co-creating your life.

It was time to seriously think about this experience. How did it apply to my life, and why was I so affected? I chose journaling to begin my work. Journaling is a wonderful tool to help you in this kind of work because you can go back and remember clues you may have received in the past but did not fully understood at the time. I began this process by asking for guidance from my higher Self, and then I followed the clues that came up.

The scarab helps you as you do this journal work by pushing up memories and dreams from the past for you to work with. The more clues you can remember, the easier it is for you to connect the dots. Just the act of writing them down and pondering them gives this process the conscious attention it needs to gestate and finally reveal their meaning so the healing can begin. Your higher Self knows you consider it important enough to pay attention. This allows for communication between your ego and your unconscious that can now become a working relationship. In this mindful state, you are attending wisdom.

I started to look back over my life and I remembered a series of hints and experiences that I thought could be related to this one. I remembered when I was thirteen years old how upset I was when the Berlin Wall went up. Although I am not German, the wall upset me to the point that I was compelled to read all the stories and magazine articles about people who had risked their lives trying to escape across the boarder between East and West Germany.

These stories affected me so much I even mentioned this in my junior high English class at school. Our English teacher had asked us to make one wish and tell it to the class. Everyone was wishing for things they wanted. I was in the last row, and when it got around to me, I told the class I wished the Berlin Wall would come down. My teacher was so impressed by my answer that it made me remember this experience. Now as I wrote it down in my journal as one of my clues, I realized that even at that young age of thirteen, part of me wanted to become whole, with no barriers or threats to wholeness.

Many years later, in my early thirties, I had a dream experience that confirmed the experience I had at age thirteen. I had come home from work with a very painful stiff neck. I layed down on my bed and fell asleep. I was awakened by the sound of a woman's voice speaking directly into my ear. She only said one word, and that was *"Berlin"*. It jolted me awake because the sensation of this was so real. Now looking back on it symbolically, I know it was a big clue. My painful stiff neck was like a wall that separated my head (consciousness) from my body (the unconscious). At the time of this dream, the literal Berlin Wall was still standing, and I had not made any connection with this symbol for myself. I did write it down though and remembered it vividly. Sometimes it takes years to connect the dots.

I can remember so clearly watching the news on the night the Berlin Wall finally did come down. I was glued to the TV as I watched the drama happening for the whole world to see. Interestingly, I observed two different reactions happening, and I could identify with both of them. On the West Berlin side, people were spontaneously taking sledgehammers to the wall as if they couldn't wait to tear it down. It had been a violation to them for too long. On the East Berlin side, however, I saw some East Berlin soldiers whose job it had been to patrol and guard this wall all these years. They stood looking on in disbelief as the wall they had been patrolling was being torn down before their eyes. I sensed for them there was something frightening and possibly even threatening about what was happening. What a drama we saw on that day as history was being made! For the German people, the work of rectification and healing, and the beginning of wholeness and unification could finally begin.

So how did all this relate to me? I started to think of how I was raised in a very rigid and judgmental religious fundamentalist up-bringing. I was taught black and white thinking, with an impenetrable wall in-between. I was taught to believe that our beliefs were the only true beliefs and everyone else's were wrong. If others did not eventually accept our beliefs, they would go to hell. If I did not believe these beliefs, I myself would go to hell. It is hard to see much difference between this thinking and the Nazi or rigid communist mentality with the wall-building compensations that resulted.

History is full of horrific examples of how this rigid, poisoned thinking has destroyed lives and whole cultures. I think of the many Holocausts, such as the Inquisition, with its nine million recorded witch killings, the millions of Jews, and other ethnic peoples who were systematically killed by Nazi's and others. I think of our own country with centuries of cruel, inhumane, and dismissive treatment of Native Americans, African slaves, and Native Hawaiians by people who thought they had a god-given right to be in total control. The justification was that we would force our beliefs on them and this would somehow save their souls.

Although I rejected this kind of dogma in early adulthood, the roots of this rigid, judgmental poison were still in my unconscious. If I did not learn to recognize it and deal with it, it would govern my psyche, and I would not even know it. I had to realize there was indeed a Nazi major general in my unconscious psyche. This is the sin passed down to the sons and daughters of the third and fourth generation. Now the scarab begins his work, going to battle for the purpose of raising consciousness with the help of the little man in my soul who also works in the underground of my psyche to help in this soul work.

The battle needed to start with the process of breaking down the wall my ego consciousness patrolled to maintain the status quo. I could no longer go back to sleep now that I had the mirror of symmetry reflecting my soul. It could no longer be just an ego agenda. It was time for the alchemist in myself to attend the wisdom I was being shown.

Carl Jung, in his book *"Memories, Dreams, and Reflections"*, describes a scarab experience of one of his patients. His patient was not making much progress in her analysis work until one day she came and told Jung a dream she had. In her dream, she saw a scarab-like beetle trying to get in the window. As she told Jung the dream, they heard a scratching sound at the window, and there behind them was a scarab-like beetle trying to get in the window. This is the mirror of symmetry, and synchronicity. This was the moment that helped his patient recognize that it is not all about ego consciousness; it's about becoming whole. From this point on, she started to make real progress with her scarab's help.

In some cultures, it is the shamans and shamanesses who take on this scarab work for their people. Some shamans have been known to wear scarabs around their necks as they go into trance to seek the symbols that can become the healing image needed to bring their patient back to health and balance. Before they could do this however, these shamans had to do the work within themselves so they could then help others. In some ways, this was the role Carl Jung had to play as he helped his patients. He was their shaman. Working with the scarab, he helped them find the symbols that would become their key to working towards wholeness.

Wisdom throughout the ages has been recognized as a feminine archetype with many names. In the <u>Jerusalem Bible</u>, she is known as Sophia. Wisdom is essential to this process. Unfortunately, for many in Western culture, she is either rejected, neglected, or forgotten. In my religious up-bringing, she was never mentioned. She was however, the one who had spoken the word *"Berlin"* in my ear to wake me up. She was essential to my process.

Now I call her Mother Wisdom. Her motto is "I unite all," and she can work with us to make this happen. As she unites, she transforms and mediates. She has been called the eternal feminine and the World Soul. In the <u>Book of Wisdom</u> in the <u>Jerusalem Bible</u>, she is described this way.

> Wisdom 7:26 read's "She is a reflection of the eternal light, untarnished mirror of God's active power, image of his goodness."

So she is that reflective mirror of symmetry we all need to look into in order to learn wisdom and understanding.

There is another quote from the <u>Book of Wisdom</u> about Sophia that is very relevant at the beginning of this new age, found in Wisdom-8:7, 8:

"Virtues are the fruit of her labors, since it is she who teaches temperance and prudence, justice and fortitude; nothing in life is more serviceable to men than these," "…Or if you are eager for wide experience, she knows the past, she forecasts the future; she has foreknowledge of signs and wonders, of the unfolding of the ages and the times."

King Solomon writes, "The desire for wisdom leads to sovereignty." What is sovereignty? It is independent, outstanding, and of supreme authority. This is an authority that needs to be present within our-selves, not a belief system that is forced on us from outside ourselves. It is related to freedom and authenticity. We need this, and we need her if we are going to break down the walls that have become barriers to our healing process individually and collectively. We first need to realize that we need to be made whole.

I know I have done a lot of wall-busting work, but it is not without the help of Sophia, the scarab, and my higher Self. I know too that I have discontinued the wall patrolling, and I feel I have celebrated the beginnings of unification within myself. Most important to me is the open communication between my conscious and unconscious and my higher Self that makes my life meaningful. This is a healing process. I no longer worry about dogma that threatens autonomy and beliefs that do not include my experience of them. What I seek is that which truly nourishes life and attends wisdom. In this way, I can experience the feeling of being fully engaged in the present as it unfolds. I am always learning and try to be mindful of my experiences.

There is a song in Handel's *Messiah* that speaks to me with affect every time I hear it. It almost brings tears to my eyes. If I am hearing it at home, I sing along from my heart. It is a passage from the Bible that goes, "Every valley shall be exalted, and every mountain and hill made low, the crooked straight, and the rough places plain".

It is sad that as one who was raised on the B-I-B-L-E, and having it pounded into me as a belief system, that somehow it was lost on me that this is a life-time experience we must live. This is a song about scarab work and the pushing up of consciousness.

No one enjoys this work, but if there are not enough people willing to do it, the accumulated consciousness of the ages and the wisdom we have yet to learn could be lost. It will be replaced by rigidity, compulsive behaviors, additions, and a complete giving over to technology. Worst of all, we could lose our very souls.

We do not need tons more information; we need understanding. Our problems today are too complex for black-and-white thinking. Solutions to our problems cannot be ego-centric. They need to be balanced in the heart-center. We need to make our priorities those that sustain us all, not just in this generation but for all the generations to come.

A few things that stand out in my religious upbringing was how totally negating and dismissive we were when it came to other people's contributions to wisdom, understanding, and quality of life. It often showed an arrogance and ignorance that only considered themselves. The other negation was a lack of respect for the sacredness of nature. With this wall down, I am grateful to be able to learn from others wisdom and Mother Nature once again with all my heart.

One of the biggest problems with our cultural myth is that it has this need to dominate. We have done it with nature and with other cultures and peoples. We act like an invasive species that, once introduced, takes over and wipes out the indigenous species. I hope this can change. All life is sacred, and we need to begin to understand this and celebrate it. If we don't begin to understand this, our own children will begin to think of themselves as worthless and life as meaningless.

Learning what sustains and nurtures life for the good of all is the direction we need to go. The harm and imbalance of the old-school way of thinking will take time to bring back into balance. Major directional change with our values and priorities is not just logical but also spiritually and psychologically imperative. We do not have the luxury of time on our side either. Mother Nature is making her messages loud and clear - grow up or burn out.

I have a friend who was a sixth -grade teacher in a rural public school. She pushed to establish what is called "outdoor school" for her science classes. She tried to incorporate ecology and conservation into her class. She soon found it is not easy teaching values that are not culturally supported. When we as a culture are making poor choices, our children become fragmented and defeated because they can see that these issues are not being addressed. Mother Nature is trying to show us our imbalance, and we need to wake up, or nature's justice will be served.

There is a saying that when the hundredth monkey learns something, somehow all the monkeys of the world know it. I hope this is true for humans too, and I hope it happens soon. If the scarab is part of our DNA, maybe we will be able tap into this. If we do, we will experience the warrior aspect because we will be battling real battles inside and outside of ourselves.

I appreciate a prayer that I have heard the first peoples of North America pray. They pray that they "might walk in beauty on this earth." Amen to that! I want to thank peoples around the world who have had this prayer and held these values even when their lands were taken from them and then treated with disrespect. I hope your cultures will be appreciated once again and respected for your wisdom you never let go of.

One of the most beautiful examples of scarab work and conscious raising being done on a collective scale recently was the movie _Black Panther_. All the ingredients of the scarab at work was in this movie. In the beginning, there was an abandoned inner-city child who had been left behind and not in a position to know his full potential. Then there was a hierarchy that somehow justified this. This collective ego agenda may have started with good intentions, but it had become control oriented.

Along comes the scarab, a warrior-like, rebellious leader who is a real ego agenda disrupter. At first, he appeared to be the villain in the eyes of the establishment. He knows that the system is imbalanced and challenges it. He finally becomes the leader, and I found it interesting that he is then shown seated on a throne that is in the shape of a scarab.

He wages war on the old school leadership, and there is a time of true chaos. In one scene, we see a charging rhinoceros. This is what it might feel like in the midst of this chaos. The rhinoceros, like the unicorn in mythology, is in the paradoxical hidden third of symmetry. He can be either deadly and extremely negative or, as in so many myths, extremely positive if he is "tamed in the lap of a virgin." In this movie the charging rhinoceros stops short and calmly lies down in front of the young priestess of the tribe. No one else would have been able to tame this wild beast.

Sophia, goddess of wisdom, is the virgin aspect we need in this process. She has the virgin wisdom needed to heal the ego imbalance and the chaos. There are many pictures in centuries past that have shown the Virgin Mary in this capacity, with a unicorn resting in her lap. We need within ourselves the virgin, the handmaiden of God, to help us through this process. If the meaning of this is not recovered, the chaos could be disastrous. If the meaning is found, there is the promise of a new day.

There is one scene where this new scarab king is standing before a panoramic view of a beautiful African sunrise, simply taking in the beauty. This is the sunrise the scarab has pushed up, and it heralds a new day after the dark night of the soul.

The movie *Black Panther* had a totally black cast of actors and actresses. They certainly proved to old-school Hollywood establishment that they had a deep pool of talent that was finally getting a chance. This also tells me though that this is still in the unconscious and not yet integrated collectively. There is much work to do, but the good news is that the scarab has begun his work.

Individuals and cultures around the world are soul-searching right now. Certainly, we in America are having to go down into our roots and see the old patterns and values that have caused much pain and dysfunction. If we don't participate both individually and collectively, we lose. If we fully participate though, we have the promise of a beautiful new sunrise and an America that truly lives our values.

Interestingly, at this time, we as Americans are confronted with a choice. We can latch onto the idea of caging children and building walls that separate us, or we can look in the mirror of symmetry and go the way of Lady Liberty. Let's do the work; our children depend on it. This is something we as Americans should be able to agree on.

CHAPTER 10

The Scarab in the Hidden Third

"One should pay attention to even the smallest crawling creatures, for these too may have a valuable lesson to teach us." Black Elk

W E HAVE LEARNED THAT ONE of the things we find in the hidden third of symmetry is the scarab. We saw this in the chapter on seeing in symmetry. From seemingly out of nowhere, there he was, shining like the sun. So, I was not surprised to find the scarab coming out of the center of so many pictures after they were placed in symmetry. It is not surprising either that the scarab is a sacred symbol in many creation myths. Perhaps I can show you why.

PLATE 1 CHAPTER 10

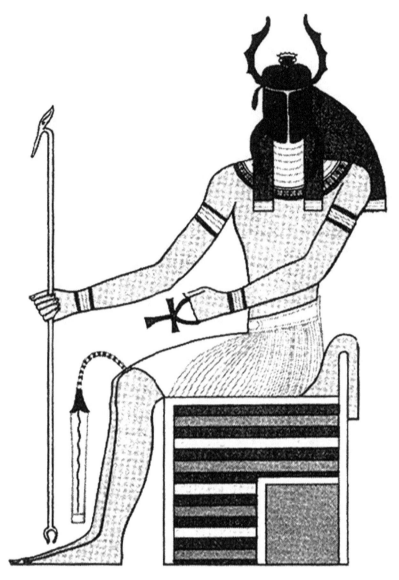

"Egyptian god Khepera holding an ankh".*

In ancient Egyptian culture, the scarab is related to the sun and its movements. The Egyptian god Khepera is pictured wearing a scarab mask. *Khepera* means to exist or to come into existence. He was a symbol of the renewal of life and its cycles. Khepera was also known as the rising and setting sun and a symbol of birth, death, and rebirth. No wonder he was such an important symbol to the ancients. In **PLATE 1 CHAPTER 10**, he holds an ankh, which is a symbol of life.

I have seen the scarab coming into, out of, and highlighted in so many pictures that I have taken inside the Earth and on the Earth, that it made me realize that the scarab is part of the Earth's DNA of life. We do not see him because he is in the hidden third of symmetry.

With the scarab, darkness and illusion are dispersed, and the light of consciousness is brought into the world. Through his work, life is transformed by creative energy. I often see him in my pictures with the symbol of a butterfly, which is a symbol of death and transformation.

I would like to show you how and where he makes his movements from the down under in the hidden darkness, which is the domain of the Mother, to pushing up the sun, and bringing back the light through the hidden third of symmetry.

* Image by ©Dover Press

PLATE 2 CHAPTER 10

"The earth swallows the sun".

PLATE 2 CHAPTER 10 shows what, in my imagination, looks like the down-under phase of the sun and the life of Khepera in the process of being rejuvenated before he is reborn. This is the sun/son in the womb of Mother Earth, and from this pyramid-shaped mound representing her womb, we see the scarab pushing the sun upward and out of this dense matter.

This can be experienced psychologically, both individually and collectively, at times when we are at our weakest and most vulnerable and when our light seems to have gone out. The theme here is "My God, why hast though forsaken me?"

Two-thirds of the way up, in the center, we can see the butterfly showing us a transformation is taking place. This butterfly appears ready to fly. Opposites are coming together in the symbol of the ankh. I can see the oval with the stem beneath it. The circle is the feminine, and the stem is the masculine; together, they symbolize life. It also looks like one of the Egyptians most sacred amulets, the *tjet*, which represents the womb or what was called the matrix of Isis the goddess as the Great Mother.

I am used to looking at these images, so I will point out that at the bottom of the ankh, I see the head of a sow facing forward, which is the death aspect of the feminine. We will see the sow over and over in these pictures. I can also see the dancers on either side of the sun as it appears to be reborn. This is the dance of death and life. There is a rebirth happening, and this too is part of the cyclical nature here on Earth. In symmetry, nature displays a drama that has been played out since the beginning of creation.

If you reverse this picture, you will see the sun rising up out of the lotus womb with the help of the scarab that finally emerges near the top.

From *The Book of Symbols* by Tascheu, I read, "As the evening star, it lead the sun into the jaws of the earth for its nightly self-sacrifice." This is what this picture looks like symbolically, particularly since we have collectively been experiencing the death of the astrological age of the sun in Pisces. Perhaps it feels like we are experiencing the death and rebirth pains of the sun in Aquarius through the precession of equinoxes. Two snakes in blue appear to come up like a caduceus with wings at the top and the sun in the middle. This is the hermaphroditic healing image we all know. A work is being done. We need to remember this when we are experiencing our own self-sacrifice or feeling that what was once a living part of ourselves is now dying or lost.

In this picture, we see the union of opposites in all kinds of ways as this drama is unfolding. The key players at work here are Mother Earth, the sun, the scarab, the mother sow, the butterfly, and the ankh. This union, according to the Egyptians, was the way in which eternal life and rejuvenation was granted to the gods. In the imagination of many cultures around the world, this is the time we must go through just before the new sun is pushed up on the new winter solstice. This is why symbolically Christmas was put at this time of the year.

In Chinese wisdom, the scarab is a symbol of the work we need to do in the process of becoming conscious and spiritually mature. This also fits with the teachings of the alchemists and the in-depth psychology of Carl Jung as well.

The sun has always been related to consciousness and the process of becoming conscious. The scarab is indispensable in this process. Khepera was also known as the "only begotten son." I find this interesting because Christ too, at the beginning of the age of Pisces, was also called the "only begotten son." In early Christianity, self-knowledge was considered the road to the knowledge of God.

Carl Jung, in his book *Psychology and Alchemy*, writes, "Salvation does not come from refusing to take part or running away. Nor does it come from just drifting. Salvation comes from complete surrender, with one's eyes always turned to the center." Jung also wrote, "We are challenged to become conscious of what presses up into consciousness from the dark unconscious." This is the role the scarab plays, helping us in this work of becoming conscious. It sometimes feels like a real ordeal, but the scarab is also a warrior, and he is willing to fight with us. This is the important work of the renewal of our hearts and minds. By doing what I call the scarab work, we no longer evade our true destiny.

Scarabs are often pictured with large horns. This is what they use to do battle. My scarab even had guns and holsters. Who knows how your scarab will show up? He will fight illusions and denial and call out the avoidance techniques of our egos. Don't be surprised if you see him in a dream. Stay in your center and work with him. He helps us through this dense dark material of our unconscious, to find the gold.

The scarab is often pictured wearing a crown on his head. The scarab's path is the royal road of the Self. He regally represents the higher purpose of our lives that the ego needs to be aligned with if we are to experience the divine in ourselves. This is the sacred path of the center in our hidden third.

I will show you this down-under process in some of the pictures I have taken and placed in symmetry. It is a path that transforms, so we will see how he is related to the butterfly with healing in his wings, the caduceus.

PLATE 3 CHAPTER 10

"With Mother Sow".

I mentioned Mother Sow in the last picture, but in **PLATE 3 CHAPTER 10**, she stands in all her regal glory. This is from a cave picture, and caves are her domain. She was to the ancients the ruler of the underworld and was known as "the white diamond sow." She was a triple goddess, and in this role as ruler of the underworld, she reclaims in death and then gives birth again.

In this picture, we see her white sow's head, and she appears to be standing like an axis, studded with diamonds. She is not alone though. From below and above, we can see the path of the scarab in its process of death and rebirth. One of the scarabs is at her feet, and one is at her face. It's as if the scarab is her son. If you look at her in profile, we can see her other two faces directed outward from the center face. This is showing her triple goddess nature. She has been given many names around the world: the Fates, the Moerae, the Graeae, the Norns, the Gorgons, and many others.

I have known people who have had near-death experiences where they found themselves in a place with three women' who were hovering over them, and in some cases, they would send them back into their present life again because they had not finished what they came to do. One man told me of his experience. The only other person he had told was his doctor, and his doctor told him he was not the only one who had a story like his.

This gentleman at age ninety-six wanted to tell me his story. He said at about age sixty, he was in the hospital and had died and found himself in a place with three women hovering over him. They said he had to go back into his life again because his work was not yet done.

It was a comfort to him now at age ninety-six because he felt that his work was now done and that at this point in his life, he was ready to go. He was not afraid of facing death. These three women are the triple goddesses. This same story has been told by many people in near-death experiences.

At her feet, we can also see the image of the face of a bat. The bat is the totem of the death aspect of the masculine principle. This is the original batman. Perhaps because of the bat's connection with caves and the underworld, we are not surprised to see him here. Together, the sow and the bat are the keepers of the abyss or the pit. I see the bat's image often in symmetry in relation to the owl as well. The owl is another totem of the death aspect of the goddess.

In the Christian tradition, it was the three Mary's who remained at the foot of Jesus's cross to receive his dead body after his crucifixion. It was one of these Mary's, Mary Magdalene who announced to the disciples that "he has risen." This is an archetypical pattern.

In John Michell's book _New Light on the Ancient Mystery of Glastonbury_, we are told an old Welsh legend about the beginnings of the new age of Pisces when Christianity was first established in Glastonbury, England. One of the founding fathers of this church, Galasteing, was looking for a location to build the church. He followed a wandering mother sow to the final location, where she finally lay down and nursed her piglets. They later called it "Sow's Way to Glastonbury." This sow became known as the "Old Church Sow." There are a number of Welsh tales like this, where clergy are led as if by magic to a new location by a mother sow, where they then build a monastery.

I saw a white diamond shape standing stone in Avebury England that had the face of a sow in profile. It was one of the largest standing stones in Avebury. Maybe she is making an appearance again for this new age.

There are those of us today who are searching for the new sacred place of this new age. We may have to follow the mother sow and her scarab through her womb or what has been called the hiding place of the pig until we can find that sacred place of the heart to begin this new age in a sacred manner. Perhaps we will find this sacred place within ourselves.

This picture of the White Diamond Sow, can be seen on my website at **www.cherylcaine.com**.

PLATE 4 CHAPTER 10

"A Mexican mural".

PLATE 4 CHAPTER 10 is a mural in Mexico. I would say that a descendant of the first peoples of Mexico painted this amazing mural. We see the bat at the bottom in the underworld and the spirals going into and out of life. The bat's head seems to be superimposed over a butterfly image, symbolizing a transformation. The sun on top appears to have been pushed up by a small scarab-like image. What a beautiful mural! We can even see the starry heavens behind the sun as if announcing a new day.

I have seen *National Geographic* magazine articles about Aztec archeological diggings. They unearthed a ceremonial burial with a man wearing a gold bat mouthpiece above his mouth, and he was buried with a woman who represented the death aspect of the feminine counterpart, the owl. These symbolic connections with nature were understood at one time.

PLATE 5 CHAPTER 10

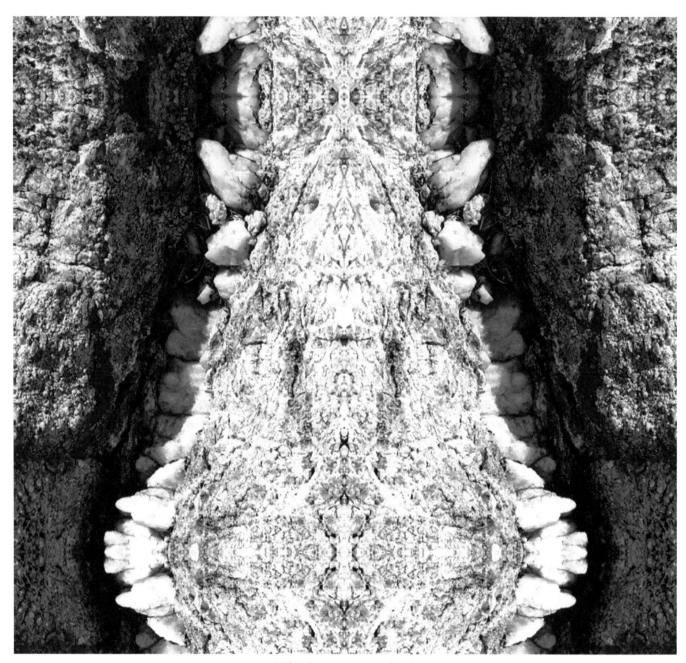

"The devouring mother".

In **PLATE 5 CHAPTER 10**, we see the Earth as a huge jawbone devouring and reclaiming back into herself. Within this jawbone, we can see the scarab fearlessly pushing his way up. The top of the jaw appears like a pyramid shape, which is the earth's womb. The scarab is climbing up through the middle of this pyramid. There is the AV superimposed over each other here as well. This is the yin yang of nature.

The center of her face appears like an ankh, with the stem going down through the middle. I can also see two other faces in profile on either side telling me she is a triple goddess. I can see the two snakes of the caduceus curving inward half-way up. This is all a very natural process going on around us all the time, unless you factor in the man-made waist and poisons that we are dumping into the earth and the ocean that take tens of thousands of years to break down. Then the process begins to be very unnatural. Our Mother Earth must not be made into a dumping ground for our over-indulgent and dysfunctional age. We will have to learn to live sustainably and remember that other generations come after us.

We can see the hermaphroditic nature of this picture, containing both the masculine and feminine within itself. This is the characteristic of the hidden third. This is the archetypal nature of all life. In psychology, we learn that there is within us the opposite within our psyche's, hidden from us unless we learn to relate to it and work with it. Carl Jung called it the anima and the animus, and they are also indispensable in the process of doing our soul work.

Etched in her two sides just below her head are the letters A and V again. They could also be a M with a hooked X symbol. This was an important symbol of the Knights Templar, and the Freemasons. I would imagine most symbols of any importance are reflected by mother nature. The letter A is also the birth letter in the Greek alphabet. Interestingly enough, it is also the letter given as the alternative name for the River Styx, which was the river in the underworld that took people into their afterlife to be reborn. This whole picture is in the shape of an A.

Reversed, we see the royal king with his scepter or sword. Mother Earth was the king maker, and she was the one who granted kingship. I think of the lady of the lake and Excalibur, in the King Arthur tales. The king was married to the land, and his queen represented the land.

I think also of the story of Jonah and his sojourn in the belly of the fish before Jonah was spat up again onto dry land. He was then finally ready to live his true destiny. Some of us will have to make a sojourn like this before we can finally accept our destiny. As Jonah learned, going in the opposite direction of our destiny does not work.

PLATE 6 CHAPTER 10

Along the Snake River.

PLATE 6 CHAPTER 10 is a natural symmetrical reflection of the Snake River. We have to look at it from a vertical angle rather than the natural horizontal angle. It's not the River Styx, but it shows through symmetry the sword and caduceus, with the HAH representing the feminine principle in the middle. Reversed, it is HVH, which is the masculine counterpart. That makes it HAVH as nature's divine trigram. At the top is the chalice, with the sword going through it. Also, at the top is the ankh, with the oval of the feminine and the stem of the masculine. These are symbols of the uniting of opposites. In my imagination, I can see the scarab near the bottom and again near the top.

Everything is yin and yang and the idea is to keep them in balance. Perhaps in the chaos of this in-between time of the ages, when the balance has been lost, we will be seeing some real upheaval until we can reclaim this natural balance once again. Before this can happen, the scarab will have to do his work and push up the sun consciousness for a new day.

PLATE 7 CHAPTER 10

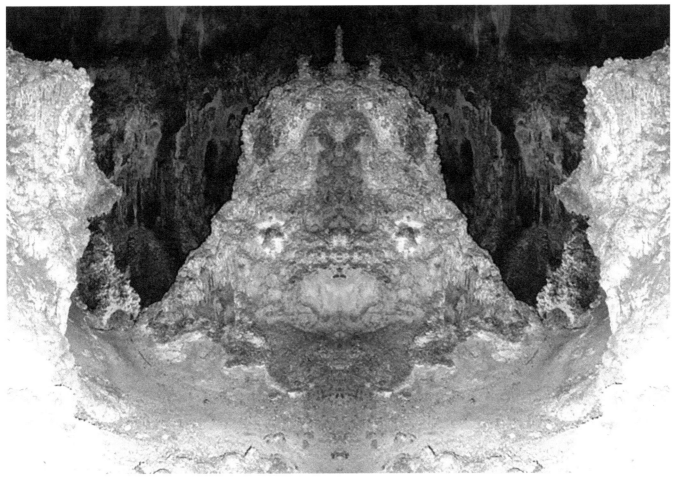

"In the underworld".

Another underworld cave picture placed in symmetry shows the white sow again on either side in profile, facing inward to the center. In the center, we have what looks like the head of a wise old man, but there are signs that he is related to the scarab.

There is an alchemical picture of the scarab that shows the scarab surrounded by an Ouroboros snake swallowing its tail. What this symbolizes from J. E. Cirlot's book, _A Dictionary of Symbols_ "is symbolic of time and of the continuity of life." "It is a variant of the symbol of Mercury," the hermaphrodite who carries the caduceus representing the coming together of opposites. The Ouroboros has been described as a dragon, and it is also symbolic of "self-fecundation or the primitive idea of a self-sufficient Nature," which "continually returns, within a cyclic pattern to its own beginning." I am not sure if it is such a primitive idea when I see these symbols so often displayed in nature's symmetry. It may just be forgotten ancient wisdom. Since this Ouroboros plays an antagonistic role in relation to the sun hero, the scarab here again must do battle to overcome death.

There is a T with a ladder-like base going up the front his body. This is like an alchemical picture too. Perhaps this is showing the ascension taking place. Behind this central figure, it looks like a womb image. In Celtic myth, the white sow was the goddess whose name meant "womb" or "hiding place of the pit." This was considered the domain of the "sacrificed god." The sacrificial death always came before the resurrection.

In some of the old Christian European churches, this pit was called the "Holy Ghost hole." On Ascension Day, a statue of Jesus was drawn upwards out of this pit. Without Barbara Walker's wonderful reference books, I would have never heard of these things. Walker is a true ancestor to someone like myself, who needed to understand and learn things I could not get anywhere else. She did her work and passed it down so we would not have to do our work alone. Thank you, Barbara Walker.

PLATE 7 CHAPTER 10 also has the appearance of the sun boat that took the old sun in to be rejuvenated and then released it again, reborn. The two fiery figures look like sun disks on either side facing the center. On the very top, we see the distinct face of the bat once again, telling us this is the underworld pit.

PLATE 8 CHAPTER 10

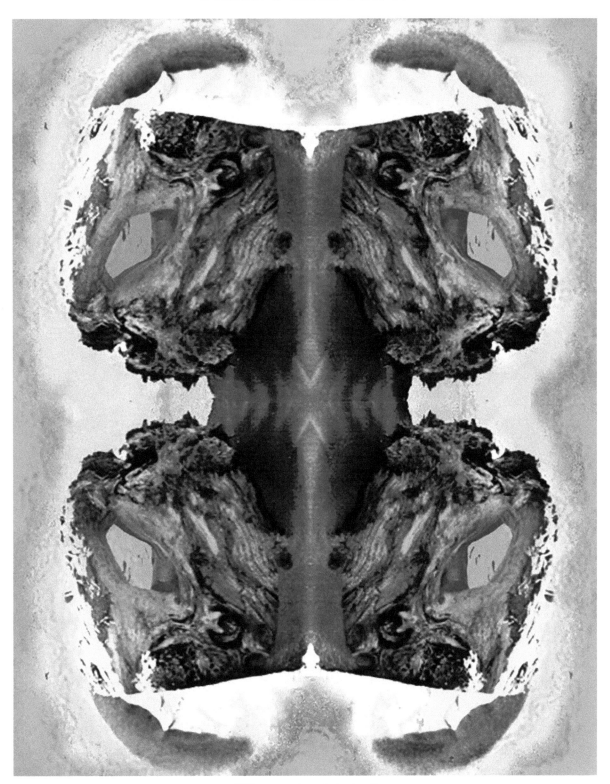

"The scarab reclaiming".

PLATE 8 CHAPTER 10 of the scarab shows his down-under aspect as well. We see the Ouroboros nature of it as it appears to be devouring itself. This picture was taken on the beach, where you often see empty shells and dead sea creatures washed up on the shore. At the very bottom, we can see a chalice with an arrow going through it. Horizontally we see V on top and A at the bottom.

PLATE 9 CHAPTER 10

"The sun boat".

PLATE 9 CHAPTER 10 is the closest thing I have to the transformational sun boats journey. For me, it is also a grail image. In the grail is the pyramid of the womb in the shape of an A. Two doves and two snakes grace the center top of this grail. The literal butterflies in this picture are telling us there is a transformation going on. On this reversed side, it looks like the transformation is going on in the head of the masculine principle.

PLATE 10 CHAPTER 10

"The sow with the ball with wings".

PLATE 10 CHAPTER 10 is another version of the "white diamond sow." In this case, the diamond is her shape. We can see her triple aspect with the faces in brown turned out on either side. When I look at this image, I think of the no-nonsense ball with wings that signaled the "end of the game" in the *Harry Potter* stories. As we look at her here, there is a definite feeling of "game over." In the center is the golden ball, and on either side are the wings, going out to the edge of the picture in both directions.

When you look at the picture on its horizontal side, we see she is not alone. There is the scarab, making his way on either side through the middle. There is an ascension-like quality to it as well. The top scarab has horses going out on either side in blue. This makes him also the charioteer. There is a fiery sun-like feel to this chariot. Perhaps our sun hero here has triumphed!

Her face appears in the shape of a throne. Here again, she grants kingship. In her very center in white on top, I see the Buddha-like figure with a cone-shaped hat on. On the lower center, we see the bat's head and his wings going out on either side. This is Mother nature's version of the Mexican mural in plate 4. We see the spirals on all four sides as well.

We will see more of the charioteer in this book.

97

PLATE 11 CHAPTER 10

Prima Materia & the Scarab

PLATE 11 CHAPTER 10 shows us the aspect of the primordial mother that the alchemist called prima materia. Prima materia is the dense base material that the alchemist starts with in their work of making gold. In the beginning of the process, the scarab is trapped in this dense material. In this picture, I see the blue scarab appearing as if trapped in the center of this dense material.

Barbara Walker gives a quote attributed to the scarab Khepera: "I laid the foundation in Maa, the primordial." Alchemists used the scarab in diagrams with a double spiral path to the center of the universe. Superimposed over this scarab is what looks like the sun disk. Perhaps we see the ball with wings here again. In the center of this scarab is the same design that is found both on the Aztec sacrificial Olin bowl, and the center of the Aztec calendar stone.

PLATE 12 CHAPTER 10

The Olin bowl 'Aztec design'

The meaning of the design image on the Olin bowl was movement, as in the movement of the heart beating. On **PLATE 12 CHAPTER 10**, turned on its side, we can see the heart, both upper and lower, in purple and blue. The sun too is connected with the heart center. I see this same design all the time in symmetry. It also has within it the trigram of HAVH. The big H is in the center, and the A and V are above and below the center. The face of the king or god was often placed in the center as in plate 18 chapter 10.

PLATE 13 CHAPTER 10

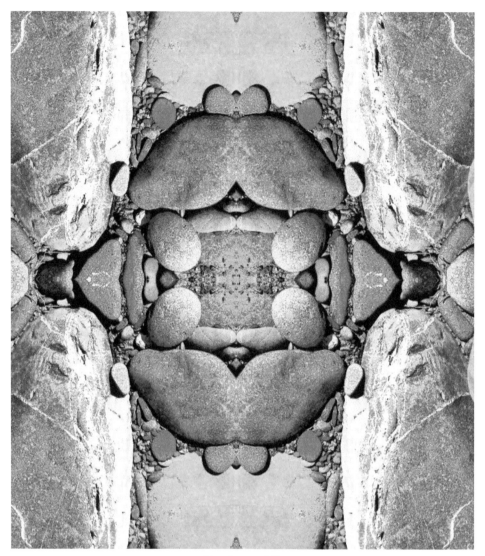

"In the rock".

PLATE 13 CHAPTER 10 also shows the blue scarab in dense rock. He is pushing up the sun at the top, and at the bottom is the sun in the down-under state in the dove's womb. I can see the faces of the sun in the sun images. In the Aztec calendar, the king's face would have been carved into the center. The whole picture is in the shape of a scarab with the H, and the letter A at the top and V at the bottom in the center section. I used color enhancement to bring out the colors. We see the same sun design in the center of the picture, with two hearts on either side from the side view. We see the butterfly design just above and below the center. This is always there, showing us the transformation is taking place.

The large rocks at the top and bottom are in the shape of doves with snakes together. This is representing the womb and the coming together of opposites. There are four snakes on the sides as well, coming together in the side center, perhaps like the design on the chariot. We see, turned on its side, a smaller version of the scarabs, making his way through the Great Mother's center. In my imagination, I can see in this design the rune symbol called "fertility." This rune appears like two X's, one on top of the other and connected. According to Ralph H. Blum, in his book called _Book of Runes_, this is about the fertility of the coming together of opposites and a new beginning, in relation to the sun hero god. He tells us this rune indicates a time to "fertilize the ground of your own deliverance." This is, for the alchemist, the self-sacrifice of our old ego agendas. It then becomes the emergence of a butterfly from a closed chrysalis state.

We can also see here the superimposed symbols of A-DNA and B-DNA as they overlap in the center. Vertically, we have the feminine A-DNA and horizontally, we have the masculine B-DNA. Perhaps the four outside snakes are the double-helix strands that carry and weave this DNA. The golden center is where they cross.

PLATE 14 CHAPTER 10

The Scarab finds the gold.

You may be wondering where the gold is in this process. **PLATE 14 CHAPTER 10** shows the end product of the work, with the gold in the center and in the background on the four cross corners. The center gold shows this end product comes from the gathering from the four directions. The gold here again is found in this dense prima materia in the brown background. In the center is the ball with wings, and the two scarabs, both upper and lower, are now in this golden center. Perhaps the ball with wings in the center shows the scarab winning, as he is being set free from this entrapment. We have the A-DNA vertically and the B-DNA horizontally. I see the four snakes coming together, making the connection surrounding this DNA to make the double helix. The sun is in the center. This shows us that the purified material in always found in the center.

On its side, the design is like the Viking rune X for partnership. The sub-title of this rune is "A Gift." For the alchemist, this is the gift that comes from the partnership between the ego and the higher Self. Part of this gift is the freedom of being set free from the dense prima materia in our lives that prevented us from living our true destiny.

PLATE 15 CHAPTER 10

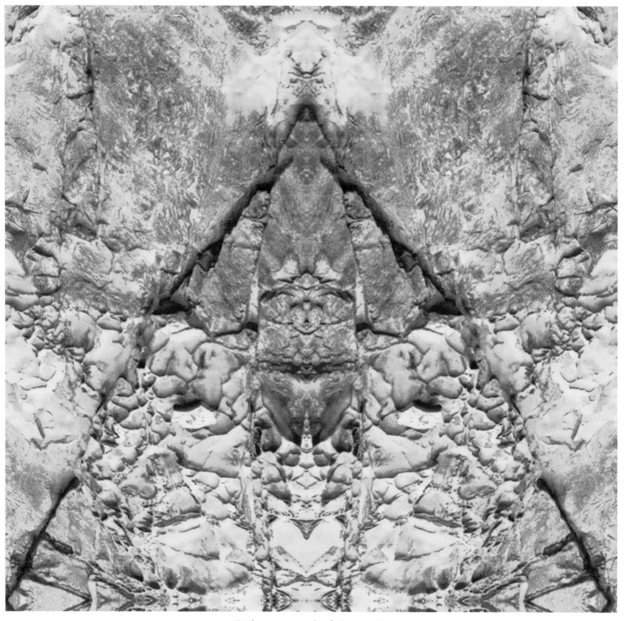

"The pyramid of the sun".

PLATE 15 CHAPTER 10 is a really good example of the feminine aspect "A" as the pyramid womb giving birth to the new sun. The scarab is in the center, with his flaming heart ascending upwards. At the bottom center, we can see the two suns facing inwards to a larger heart at the bottom of this image. There are often two hearts like this. I have seen pictures of Mary and Jesus together with their hearts exposed. I think this is related to this wisdom of Mother Natures. It has been a symbol of meditation for many. This shows the heart that the new sun received from his mother.

There are two faces at the top also facing into the center. These also could represent the two solstice suns.

PLATE 16 CHAPTER 10

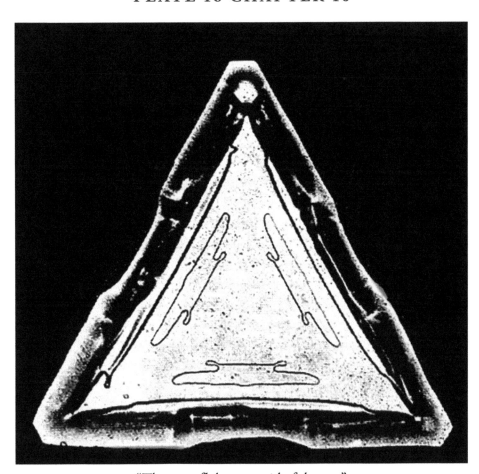

"The snowflake pyramid of the sun".

None of these themes in nature are isolated. They re-occur because they are archetypal. **PLATE 16 CHAPTER 10** shows us another of William Bentley's snow crystals. This snowflake is unique because of its pyramid design. In the center, there appears to be a female figure poised to give birth. At the top is the sun coming up, with its rays shinning down. We only see this example because of Bentley's meticulous work taking pictures of snowflakes. This is from Dover Press in the book *Snow Crystals* by William Bentley.

PLATE 17 CHAPTER 10

"The waters of life".

PLATE 17 CHAPTER 10 is taken by the Pacific Ocean shows us the scarab in relation to the water of life. Carl Jung talks about this in his book *Phycology and Alchemy -* He writes, "No water will become the elixir save that which comes from the scarab of our water." This is the source of life, and it is in the depths of our water, which is in our unconscious. It is trapped there until it is released through our heart-center and our emotions. These depths are in the hidden third that we must find and bravely go into, if we want to drink of this elixir of life. We see these waters in plate 8 chapter 2 as well.

In this plate, we see the scarab being released from the entrapment of matter as the water flows above and under him. In the new green growth beneath him, we see the chalice with the two doves and the two snakes. A caduceus appears, going up near the top, with the two snakes turning inward. The scarab appears to be meditating on the transformation taking place.

PLATE 18 CHAPTER 10

In the Vesica Piscis

PLATE 18 CHAPTER 10 shows the scarab in all its archetypal glory, with the sun shining out of the vesica piscis or the pointed oval of the womb. Barbara Walker, in her book *The Woman's Encyclopedia of Myths and Secrets*, tells us how wide-spread this symbol was. She says,

"The pointed-oval fish sign was even used by early Christians to represent the mystery of God's union with his mother-bride, which is why Jesus was called "the little Fish in the Virgin's fountain". "Sometimes Christ at his ascension was shown rising into a "heavenly vesical," as if returning to the Mother symbol. The vesica was also shown as a frame for the figures of Jesus and the saints".

This is one of Mother nature's version of this image. It is surrounded by the waters of the womb. The B-DNA – masculine is in the center, and side ways is the A-DNA of the feminine and the container of the masculine. There is a butterfly image at the bottom and the top center. The intersecting HAVH is in the center. On its horizontal side, I can see the scarab pushing up the sun in the pyramid shape near the center.

PLATE 19 CHAPTER 10

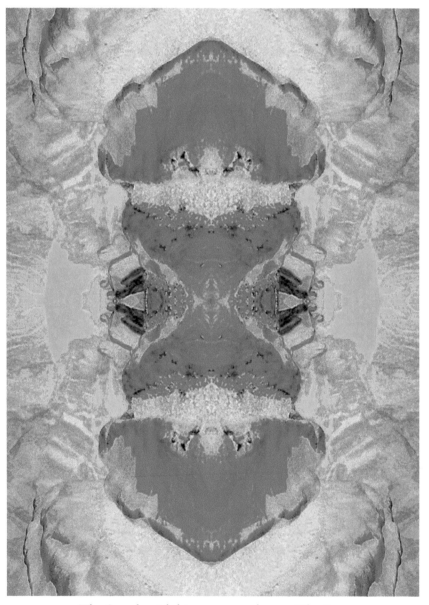

The Scarab with his crown pushes up The Sun

The royal scarab has pushed up the sun in **PLATE 19 CHAPTER 10**. His crown is studded with jewels. He also appears here in the shape of a *dorje*, which is a form of a scepter called a "diamond -holder." The diamonds show the divine masculine spirit buried within the feminine lotus. Above the scarab is the bright new sun that the scarab has just victoriously pushed up. In the very center on both sides we see the bells, which is the feminine counterpart of the dorje.

PLATE 20 CHAPTER 10

"The scarab that worked with me".

PLATE 20 CHAPTER 10 shows the scarab that worked in my depths as I processed my prima materia, and my emotions. I was doing a ceremony for myself, and in this process, I was burning pieces of paper with words and thoughts on them that represented aspects of my life that needed to either be transformed or let go of completely. This is truly a symmetrical picture of my inner self and outer selfworking together with a prayer for transformation.

I was not surprised when I saw my blue scarab warrior in the center doing his work. His long horns reach up like arms, to the healing caduceus image above him. Right there on his back was the butterfly of transformation. It feels like something from above him is reaching down to help draw him up as he pushed upwards.

On either side, we see the fire dancers. They appear like a red sickle as if saying it is time to harvest. Like the work of the alchemist, this was a time for the fertilizing of the ground of my deliverance. A sacrifice is being made so that the change can happen. There are two fiery diamond shapes below them. In the Tarot symbology, the two of diamonds represents change. The matchsticks were difficult to keep lit for very long, so I had to use a number of them. In this picture, they appeared as the six of swords. Barbara Walker, in her book _The Secrets of the Tarot_, says the six of swords represents a "passage, or a journey by water." It was likened to the passage on the River Styx that goes through the underworld, leading from a death of some kind to rebirth. This is how the scarab helps us receive the elixir of life. The sun in this picture is in the down-under phase. There appears to be a white swan on either side facing inwards near the top. Ted Andrews in his book "Animal Speak" tells us the swan's neck is a bridge to higher realms. It reminds me of the female voice that said Berlin in my ear when I was suffering from a stiff neck. The swan gives us the ability to bridge these realms. At this time transformation was starting to take place. The keynote Ted Andrews gives to the swan is: "Awakening the true beauty and power of the Self".

From the top sides these could also be white geese spiraling inward almost in a protective manner like a true mother goose. I read in Ted Andrews book Annimal Speak that "a goose as a totem can reflect that you are about to break free of old childhood restraints and begin to come into your own. How encouraging these geese were to see in this image of my transformation ceremony.

I look for these symbols after the fact, when the ceremony is over. They are not premeditated. This makes it a picture that marks where I am in my process. I look for all the symbols I can find and then try to discover what they mean. Working with the scarab is a process that cannot be controlled or rushed, it is endured. As we read in the wisdom of the I-Ching so often, "perseverance furthers," so hang in there.

CHAPTER 11

Nature's Royal Charioteer
(In the Hidden Third)

THERE IS A WONDERFUL ANCIENT Mesopotamian story that Marie Louis Von Franz tells in a documentary film series called "*The Way of the Dream*". It's a story of an ancient king charioteer whose story was found engraved on a wall. I would like to paraphrase his story for you.

When this charioteer king was a young and powerful warrior prince, he victoriously rode through his kingdom on his chariot. A star in the sky shone down on him, and everywhere he went, the people would bow down to him. I can imagine Joseph Campbell describing him at this point by saying of him, "What a good boy am I!" This describes a well-developed and vitally functioning ego. This can be a good thing indeed, and it was for this charioteer.

Later in his life though, this charioteer experienced what we might call his mid-life crisis. As he rode his chariot through the land, his star fell from the sky to the ground. Right then he knew that what he had to do now was pick up this star and carry it on his back. From this point on, his job was to serve the star.

At the beginning, when the star shone down on him from the sky, the star seemed to serve him, but now the roles were reversed. This is the point in life when the divine can impact one in a whole new way. It becomes a confrontation that forces us to alter our entire live's. He now learned that it was no longer all about his ego agenda. Now, as he went through the land, the people no longer bowed to him, they bowed to the star he carried on his back.

If we are to evolve beyond our egos, this is the activation point needed for us to realize that if we are to live our true and full destiny, we must serve something higher than ourselves. For our ego's, this can feel like a real demotion.

It is good in the first half of life to develop a well-functioning ego and be proud of our victories and accomplishments. At some point, however, our conscious ego, which depends heavily on only a few of the four dominant psychological functions, which are thinking, feeling, intuition, and sensation, begins to realize that the functions we have relied on are insufficient. In fact, if we do not acknowledge our weaker functions, realizing our ego's limitations, we cannot evolve beyond this point. If we do not become re-aligned and make this transition, we can become dysfunctional and imbalanced. To make this re-alignment, we have to become conscious of our new role, or we set ourselves up for a fall. Carl Jung would remind us that the divine is only accessed through our weakest function, which is the function totally rejected by our egos. This is why our egos must be willing to accept this new role.

In the matters of worldly success, the Tarot charioteer is warned to understand that he must be careful because "the victorious road of the charioteer could lead to hell." This was found in Barbara Walker's book *The Secrets of the Tarot*. When the Star Self is activated, it is unstoppable. Like the karmic turning of the wheel, resistance, as they say, is futile.

The ego is now to be in service of the divine Self. If this happens, there is the possibility of realizing more of our full potential and becoming a co-creator of our destiny. The hard part of this reality is now our egos can no longer take all the credit and glory for it. Our lives take on a bigger purpose and meaning though, and that makes it worth the ego sacrifice.

In the Tarot deck, the charioteer is pictured as a victorious king standing in his chariot with a four-pillar canopy of stars over his head. Like the Enlightened Ones, the charioteer is capable of bringing together the earth with the heavens, if he keeps himself aligned with the Self.

What is puzzling about this Tarot image of the charioteer is, the horses are paradoxically pictured, going in opposite directions, and the charioteer usually does not even hold the reins. The chariot he stands in is called "the triumphal car." He stands still in meditation, of the holy grail in front of him, and he knows that when the chariot starts to move, there will be no stopping him and no turning back. He leaves what his life has been, behind him. Once this star Self has been activated, it is dangerous for the ego to deny or fight it.

Barbra Walker, in her book "*The Secrets of the Tarot*," describes this charioteer as representing the "Lord of the World," and this card represents transitory earthly glory. "Like so many god kings, he was doomed to the inevitable fall after his day of glory." The message was that he too was mortal. I imagine this is true of the ruler of an age as well, like the old age of Pisces and the new age of Aquarius.

This transition from ego to Self is often activated in our late thirties or early forties, but it can happen at any time. For women, it often happens at the time of menopause. It brings with it a period of uncertainty, disorientation, and self-reflection. For some, it will be a time to let go of the dysfunction of our egos, and other people's agendas as well, that no longer serve to help us evolve but rather keeps us in our imbalance. This must happen to make the changes expected of us from our higher Self. We must learn just how naive and presumptuous our ego centeredness has made us.

It is also a time for us to accept the challenges that the Self presents to us. The path we will take in the second half of our life may be totally different from what we have lived in the past.

Like a caterpillar that wraps itself in a cocoon, waiting to become a butterfly, there is no telling what your life will be like when that chariot moves forward again. This is a transformational time in life, and the ego needs to watch, learn, listen, and be in line with the messages that come from the Self. Then the ego needs to learn to trust and act on what we learn.

In the cocoon time, the ego is protected from the spotlight until the butterfly emerges, ready to live a higher purpose. The ego may feel in this transition, like one is dropping out and life is passing them by. This too is necessary because gestation is not done in the spotlight.

In the news, we see some of our victorious modern-day charioteers as they are approaching the mid-life phase of their lives. These are the charioteers whom we, as a collective, have bowed down to. They are the victorious billionaires of our new technological age. Up to now, they have called the shots not only in our culture but around the world. Their dysfunction and naive imbalance is now starting to reveal the problems in their products and services, even to the point of personal and social loss of security and privacy. They have, in their way, unwittingly opened a Pandora's box and unleashed it on the collective. They wanted people to become addicted to their products and services, and they have succeeded in making it happen. All future generations will have to deal with these new challenges.

It is not just these technological giants though, but the whole collective that is facing a new reality, and we need to wake up to it. We have given ourselves and our children over to this, and now we need to pause and reassess where we are going. As a collective, we will have to take responsibility for the fact that life is becoming more and more dysfunctional. If we do not wake up, our identities, destinies, and freedoms are all going to be threatened. The world of technology and innovation is ruled by Aquarius, so it is not surprising that this is one of the first crises we face in this new age. On top of this, the values of the old Piscean age are dissolving, leaving us feeling vulnerable and out of control.

Like the charioteer when his star has fallen, we need to find our center again, and balance our heads with our hearts. I say "hearts" deliberately because Aquarius is about our heads and our thinking function, but the opposing sign of Aquarius is Leo, and Leo is about the heart center. For this new age, Aquarius and Leo are the two signs that we will need to balance. They are like the charioteer's horses going in opposite directions. If we do not integrate both, we will be imbalanced. Together, they can work wonderfully for the good of all. Leo rules the heart, creativity, the child self, and the needs of the individual. If we go into this new age ignoring this, these could be the casualties.

The best way to avoid this imbalance is for more individuals to be willing to pick up their star. Our egos have not been the best judge or discerning check, to keep us in balance. The ego likes black and white, right and wrong, our way or the highway. These ways are part of the old school that needs to be dropped, if we are to face the complex problems we are going to have to deal with. We as a collective need to realize that giant egos that claim to have all the answers and want total control are not going to help us through this perilous transition. The stress of this transition is strongly felt by our children. It is also very hard on those conscientious parents who are forced to be super vigilant because the world is not safe for their children. It is important to be mindful of the child self within and without.

I am encouraged to see a creative renaissance taking place in older crafts that seem to have been lost. We are learning the value of working with our hands, using tools that last generations and require hard work and discipline from the heart to bring about creative results. This is a good Leo balance to the instantaneous tools of this technological age that has outcomes with a click of the mouse and can replicate without the need for craftsmanship.

We need to be conscious also of the negative side of a Leo imbalance. It is a huge ego run amok. They would be the charioteer saying, "It's all about me." I can see major problems with either sign if things go into a real imbalance. It would be unchecked technological development with huge egos running the show.

Carl Jung called this situation "giantism." He warned that it could bring about a "universal catastrophe and a threat to consciousness." He describes giantism as a hubris of consciousness in the assertion that "nothing is greater than man and his deeds." This is a very real threat if these two signs are imbalanced and if there is a lack of discernment that does not bring it into check. It is a precarious time we live in.

Martin Luther King Jr. is the best modern example I know of, who represents a true charioteer aligned with the values of his divine destiny. As a result of his example, he became an inspiration for a whole generation. Because he was aligned with the values of his divine destiny, he was motivated from his heart (Leo) for the good of all, (Aquarius), and as a result, his life took on real meaning. His spiritual strength made it possible for him to live a legacy of hope with unwavering courage, to carry on in the face of any opposition. He knew the dangers he faced, but they would not stop him.

His message became a juggernaut that was unstoppable, and he knew that when his chariot moved, he went with it. This is why he could confidently say from his heart center on the last day of his life, "I have been to the mountaintop, and I have seen the promised land." This is the higher wisdom, the vision he saw in that divine center, and he planted that vision in all our hearts. His message is still our vision and goal in these trying times. In this new age, we have the opportunity to live this higher vision, which brings with it a unique balance of Aquarius and Leo.

We are living at a time when we are so polarized that we have lost our true center. It is always darkest before the dawn. Our leaders seem to either be afraid to lead or are operating from a gigantic ego agenda. Nevertheless, I can see a new direction on the horizon. The eloquent younger generation like those who did the "March for their lives", to draw attention to gun violence, are coming from their hearts, for the good of all, and many of them are now of voting age. They are going to insist on leaders who actually show up, and are willing to do their part for the good of all. Perhaps this is the generation that Dr. King saw in his heart's vision. Like Bob Dylan's song "For the Times, They Are A Changing", our leaders need to get out of the way if they can't lend a hand.

BE MINDFUL OF OUR CHARIOT.

We will need to be mindful of the chariot we live on—our Mother Earth. We can't ignore her or leave her in our unconscious. Care for the earth is a no-brainer, but here we are, with the symptoms of our abuse and neglect all around us. Attending to the earth is simply a return to sanity if we can learn to accept our responsibility and become her partner, rather than her destructive children. If we do not make the right choices, our children will look back on us and say, "What were you thinking?" There is no more time for denial, because the earth is giving us so many messages that are getting louder and louder, and we are setting ourselves up for a huge reality check. We will have to learn to honor our living Mother Earth.

The first peoples of this country warned us long ago, that we were going down the wrong road when it comes to taking care of our Mother Earth. There should be no question about what our children are meant to inherit from the previous generations. This is a real test of what our values are, and whether or not we are going to be a responsible people.

In the Lord's Prayer we pray, "Lead us not into temptation but deliver us from evil." This prayer is as relevant today as it ever was. It requires ego reflection and guidance from the divine. Deliverance from evil is a very real need at this time.

LET'S LOOK AT THE STAR.

Paradoxically, it takes a strong, independent ego to have the ability to serve their star. These are individuals who are capable of standing independently on their own and have disciplined themselves and prepared for the challenges they will be given. Only then can they accept their partnership with the Self, let go, and let God. These are the ego's who have faced their dragons and fears and are ready to serve. Our egos, our DNA, our life experiences, and the earth under our feet must all work together. Then we can pick up our star and be ready to go when our chariot begins to move.

We find our charioteer in the hidden third of symmetry, but the star is in the divine fourth dimension. This is the place that brings either wholeness, healing, and purpose, or destruction. Carl Jung presents some very interesting wisdom on this dimension in his book _Memories, Dreams, and Reflections_. He writes that in the experience "of the Self, it is no longer just the opposites, God, and man that are reconciled as it was before, but rather the opposites within the God image itself." This gives us a whole new look at the meaning of serving the divine, and how a human can render service to the Divine Self. This is as Jung puts it, "so the creator may become conscious of his creation and man conscious of himself."

When he talks about bringing together the opposites within the God image itself, I think of the seemingly lost and neglected sojourning divine feminine. I see so many pictures in symmetry and even just pictures in profile that show us the images together, of (Her body, and His head). It is time for this to be become consciousness.

At least in the West, we have lost the concept of the divine feminine principle and how to relate to her. As the third grader in my class said to me, "It's not Mother Nature, it's God." So, what does this mean for Mother Nature? Does this reduce her to our gross national product? When we take the sacred out of creation, we have proven, that we end up raping and trashing her. This has to change. We can no longer negate Mother Nature and the divine feminine. I can see that the God image has lost his feminine counterpart. Without her, there is no yin/yang balance. This is a tragic split!

For me, this is a way that I can contribute and be of service to the healing process that brings the divine masculine and feminine together, and at the same time helps me know myself along with my inner and symbolic nature, that to me, also represents the divine feminine. This six-cornered star in nature, is the yin/yang symbol of wholeness. We can then become the vessel of the divine feminine and masculine in a conscious way. In becoming conscious, we begin to heal the split.

Everything in life is male and female, light and dark, positive and negative. These are not judgments then, they are two halves of a whole that are both a necessary part of the balance. We have to stop thinking of them as opposites and more like two halves of a balanced whole. Like the symbol of the caduceus with the two snakes intertwined on an axis, this is a balance, that is healing. The challenge then is to become conscious. Christ said, "Man, if thou knowest what thou dost, thou art blessed, but if thou knowest not, thou art accursed and a transgressor of the law."

We thought the nuclear arms race, would be a deterrent to war, until we found that other countries want the same false sense of security and power, that we have. Now we begin to see how out of control it has become, and we don't know how it can be checked.

Carl Jung wrote, "Touching evil brings with it the grave peril of succumbing to it." This so-called positive deterrent to war can "lose its ethical character" if it ever had one. It now becomes like an addiction in which more and more is needed to maintain this deterrent. In the meantime, one wrong person in a position of power can put us all at grave risk.

It is naive of us to believe that we and our particular collective will always judge rightly, and for this reason, we cannot identify ourselves with being all good or others with all bad. We are usually unconscious of our cultural and ego prejudices. We could easily become the victims of misjudgment. It isn't until years later that we can see the error of our thinking. By then, it could be too late. With the wide spread misuse of the internet, the threat of this is even greater.

On the other side of this equation, we aspire to ideals, and dogmas that we can never hope to live up to. This can be anything, from thinking our egos can love everyone unconditionally, to the insistence of the ideal kitchen to cook in. These too can become obsessive, addictive, or impossible to live up to, and drain our energy. The big challenge of the charioteer then is, as Jung puts it, "not succumb to either of the opposites." He suggested that this would even include "optimism and pessimism." The goal is to "know thyself", carry your star, and be aware of your motives.

The biblical heroes were not chosen because they were perfect; in fact, many of them were very flawed. They are given tasks that are seemingly impossible from the ego's standpoint, yet they are given victory against all odds. It was their willingness to carry the destiny they were given that mattered, and they knew that if they would have refused, it would not have gone well for them. I remember the choice Moses was given, which was lead your people out of slavery or become a leper. This is how drastic this confrontation with the activated Self can be. The focus then is our partnership to god/goddess and the star of totality and destiny, which then must become your true motivation. It is above all else.

I will show you some of the images of the archetype of the chariot and the charioteer that I have found in the hidden third of nature's symmetry. We will also see the star of wholeness, the caduceus, and the coming together of opposites in these pictures. We will see that the charioteer too, is an archetypal pattern that reoccurs in nature.

PLATE 1 CHAPTER 11

"The snowflake charioteer".

I call **PLATE 1 CHAPTER 11** the "snowflake charioteer." This example was found in a real snowflake, from W. A. Bentley's book *"Snow Crystals"* by Dover Press. I have enlarged and dissected it to make it easier to see the details. Normally, it would not be seen by the naked eye. Keep in mind that as this picture was being taken, this charioteer was in the process of melting. What could be more temporal than a melting snowflake?

The fundamental structure of all of creation is like a mirror that shows us that what is happening within ourselves is also happening outside ourselves. The charioteer as a reoccurring pattern in nature, shows that we need to see and understand for ourselves what this means. As a mirror, nature is a source of understanding. One thing this archetype shows us is that we too are temporal.

This is a rather unique and complex snowflake, so I will point out what I am seeing. In the center is the complete enlarged but unaltered snowflake as it fell from the sky on Bentley's Vermont farm. On the upper right, we see the face of our king charioteer. I cut it out of the upper center of this snowflake. He appears as if he is wearing a crown. Also cut out of the center is a sunburst design, which tells me this was the chariot of the sun. In history and in mythology, the king's chariot often had the image of the sun at the front and center of the chariot. This sun image seems to have two different aspects. There is the down under sun that looks somewhat like a bat, which represents the down under sun, and the upper part of the sun appears like the glorious sunburst of the victorious king and the rise of consciousness.

This unique snowflake is totally different on the bottom half, where we can see a geometrically enclosed chariot with the two horses at the bottom going in opposite directions. There is a star in the very center, we see superimposed on his chin. I think this charioteer fulfilled his purpose; in fact, he will live on in Bentley's book and mine as well.

PLATE 2 CHAPTER 11   **PLATE 3 CHAPTER 11**

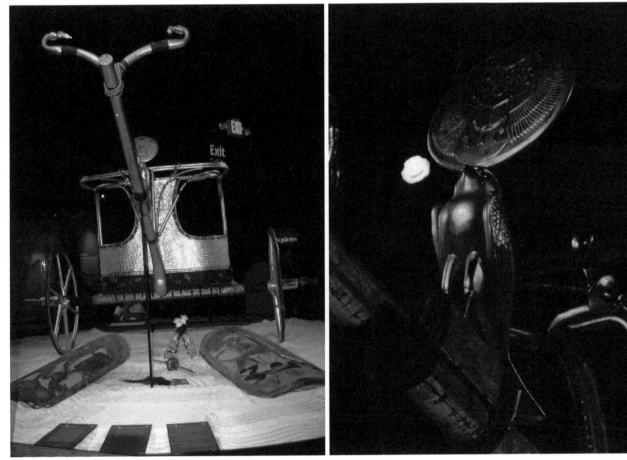

"King Tut's chariot".

I went to an exhibit of King Tut and took pictures of his chariot. Here in the front middle of **PLATE 2 CHAPTER 11**, we see the sun disk seated on the head of Horus, the sun god. In the middle of the sun disk on **PLATE 3 CHAPTER 11**, we see the scarab pushing up the sun. Since this chariot was buried in King Tut's tomb, it was his chariot in life and in his after life as well. Perhaps his chariot was to take him back to the heavens after his death. What could this mean symbolically for us, both in our physical life and in our afterlife.

PLATE 4 CHAPTER 11

"A stone sculpture in Rome, Italy".

PLATE 4 CHAPTER 11 gives us a clue about the nature of the chariot itself. It was a master craftsman of old who knew this wisdom long ago. This is in fact, the way these craftsmen passed down their wisdom. They hid it in plain sight. This is a stone sculpture in Rome, Italy, and the picture was taken by Germaine Hammon, a friend of mine.

When we look at this sculpture, we see that it is actually in profile, or as if it is one side of a symmetric whole. We see the horse's head is turned to one side away from the center. What people may not notice is that it is emerging out of the silhouette of a pregnant female figure. This is a hint that something is being birthed into this incarnation. The feminine principle is the chariot bringing forth new life.

PLATE 5 CHAPTER 11

"Plate 4 in symmetry".

PLATE 5 CHAPTER 11 is the same picture placed in symmetry. Here, we see the complete chariot in the form of the body of the feminine principle. The horses are coming out in opposite directions. We need this paradoxical opposition to our ego agenda, even if it creates pain and stress. Without it, we do not sense the need to move into our center and evolve towards wholeness. The wheels of this chariot are protruding out of her lower belly.

In the center is our shining charioteer, and his image includes the collective as well. This charioteer, like the tourists in Rome, are temporal and always changing. In another minute, he will be replaced. In the lower center, we see what represents the divine masculine, the jade herm, making this a coming together of opposites, - spirit and matter. The Chinese considered jade to be the "congealed semen of the celestial dragon," from Barbara Walker's _The Woman's Dictionary of Symbols and Sacred Objects_.

As I was writing this chapter, I saw a Public Broadcasting program on horses, and they showed a replica of an ancient Chinese chariot and how it may have been used. They demonstrated that their chariot may have been more efficient if the charioteer was on his knees rather than standing. The historian remarked, "The chariot tells you how it wants you to use it for maximum handling." This tells me the chariot has an agenda of its own, and the charioteer must learn what it is in order to work with it in the best way possible.

This can only be learned by experience. This is a good reason we should be observing nature outside and inside ourselves. This is why we need to learn to work with the DNA we have been given.

PLATE 6 CHAPTER 11

"Rocks on a beach".

PLATE 6 CHAPTER 11 placed in symmetry was taken on the West Coast. We see again the full female figure with the horses coming out in opposite directions. The axle and wheels support the chariot at the bottom. In this plate too, the charioteer is vague and temporal. His face is in the rocks, and stones on the beach that are constantly being rearranged by the waves of the sea.

On the front of the chariot, there is a black four-fold snake design that seems to be moving in a spiral motion. It is a form of a swastika, which has been a sacred symbol around the world since 10,000 BC. The design implies movement. The four-dark snakelike spirals could also be like the four-horse ancient symbol called the tetrascele that is a symbol of the sun chariot. It also relates to the Great Mother's big dipper in the northern sky, with its tail or handle marking the four seasons.

It could also be showing us the fourfold nature of earthly life, with its four basic elements air, water, fire, and earth that inform and influence us in this life. These four elements are related to the four ego functions of thinking, feeling, intuition, and sensation and the symbols of the four directions north, south, east, and west.

PLATE 7 CHAPTER 11

"Earth's chariot".

In this wonderful example of the chariot. We see the lower body of the feminine principle from her waist and hips down to the wheels. Within her center is the female chalice, with the masculine herm within, coming together in the center. This is how all life is conceived. It is always female and male.

Another characteristic of the chariot is that it can amazingly put us in the pathway, of what we need to deal with and learn in this life. If we try to avoid it, it becomes harder to deal with. If we don't learn from it, we are fated to repeat the lesson until we do. We need to remember this when we begin to see that our environment needs our attention, wherever that might be; at home, at work, in our community, and the earth itself. The chariot is one of those things that is either grounding under our feet, or it is in our face. If it is in your face, you have work to do.

If we reverse this same image, we see the enthroned and crowned king holding the ankh, like so many pictures we see Egyptian symbolism. The ankh is a symbol of the male and female coming together, and it was called the "key of life." The king is enthroned by the feminine principle.

THE TWO KINGS AND THE MOTHER EARTH

Many ancient cultures and the Kabbala have recognized two types of kings. One is the stern wartime charioteer with his sword, and the other the beneficent peace-time king with his scepter, sitting on his throne. Both the chariot and the throne represent the feminine principle. The crown of the goddess Isis is pictured as a throne. She was the "king maker." She gives the king his sword or scepter.

How different it would be if our leaders considered themselves in a sacred marriage to the land, knowing they were temporary, but the land was not. This is like the way the wise chiefs of the first peoples of our continent cared for the land. It was like a marriage.

PLATE 8 CHAPTER 11

Death of the Charioteer

PLATE 8 CHAPTER 11 shows us the death aspect of the charioteer as he finishes his work on this earth. He sits in his chariot here, and he seems to be fading into the sand on the beach. Even the horses going out in either direction are pictured as dead wood. There appears to be two buzzards on the chariot that face inward, as if telling him his time is over. The buzzard is another of the totems of the death aspect of the divine feminine that reclaims.

In dreams, the image of the horse is an important indicator of our physical health or lack of it. If you have a dream of a wounded horse, it is a warning from your body. Get to a doctor and get checked out. This tells us that our bodies are also related to our chariot.

There appears to be a crab in the middle of this image. This too is a totem of the death aspect of the divine feminine. In the center of the chalice, we see the new growth, showing the beginnings of new life. This tells us that death is not the end. There is life after death. It also shows us that there must be a sacrifice, and that something must die before new life can begin. This is not just referring to physical death but also about the death of some aspect or part of ourselves that we need to let go of before new life can begin. Like the moon, with its phases of waxing and waning, we need to be filled and emptied periodically before we can begin a new cycle. We live many lifetimes in our life.

Our body's intestines and our brains both must go through a repeated digestion process.

PLATE 9 CHAPTER 11

"The charioteer and the scarab".

PLATE 9 CHAPTER 11 shows that the charioteer and the scarab also appear to be related. Here in the top center, we see the face of the charioteer superimposed on the back of a scarab. I can see the image of his heart right under this, and there are two snakes that come together at the top of the heart like a caduceus. The horses go out in opposite directions. Near the bottom is a small star on the axil top in white at the very center. Again, (A and V) are superimposed over the center.

There is a lot of water in this picture, and the wheels are made of water. We also see the green growth coming out as if embracing life. This could be the victorious rebirth of the charioteer/scarab after he emerges out of the "waters of life."

PLATE 10 CHAPTER 11

"As the womb".

PLATE 10 CHAPTER 11 is remarkably like an image of the womb, which is also a good description of the chariot symbolically. This is not surprising because the picture was taken in a cave by the sea. Both caves and the sea are related to the womb of Mother Earth.

We can see the double dove in the two white flowers that characterize the chalice/womb. In the center is an ankh, showing the coming together of opposites and the continuation of life. There is the heart shape of the double-snake caduceus, with the snakes facing inward in the center. The snakes point to a butterfly, showing us a transformation is taking place. This shows the transformational quality of the womb.

The outer leaves outline the outer wheels of the chariot. I see two small horses facing outward in light blue just under the blossoms. In the background, it appears like the head of the masculine, again giving us the image of her womb and his head superimposed. The head is the masculine chalice of transformation and the womb is the feminie chalice. Both are capable of giving birth. I see this combination of his head and her body so many times in symmetry and in profiles in nature. The scarab is emerging at the top center of this chalice in blue, as if in the process of rebirth or emergence.

This image reversed is an image of the king enthroned. In the center bottom, we see what looks like a symbol of the omphalos, which was thought to represent the "center of the world." The top of the omphalos is in the ankh at the bottom. It is the small pyramid shape near the bottom in blue. It also appears like the scarab is climbing up from it. The omphalos was also considered to be an image of the womb. Barbara Walker tells us that it was the patriarch that changed this to mean the navel of the world.

PLATE 11 CHAPTER 11

"The Jaguar Seat at the center of the world".

The first peoples of the Southwest of North America and South America thought of this "center of the world" as the jaguar seat. I found an example of this sacred place at the Grand Canyon in Arizona. This is truly a place where the earth opens up like nowhere else, I have been. This is the place where the earth and the sky come together, and it feels like you can see forever. This is where the upper world contacts the underworld and the unconscious can become conscious within ourselves. This is a place of self-discovery and transformation. This is where we face our depths, and soar to our heights. It can also be like a place where our star falls from the sky and we must now pick it up and carry it. This is not a light-weight symbol, and it relates to the womb of the earth, feminine wisdom, and powerful energy.

When I put this into symmetry, I was amazed by what I saw. This is the chariot of the goddess herself. In mythology, the goddess is often pictured with a chariot pulled by large wild cats. In the center between the jaguars is the omphalos or womb center, and the two jaguars face outward. Jaguars are creatures of the night. According to shamanic traditions, the jaguar is related to the underworld, which is the domain of feminine wisdom. It is the place where the night sun resides. Perhaps in the dark green at the bottom here, the scarab sits dormant, waiting to be rejuvenated and make his ascent once again.

The ancients had wisdom that we have yet to learn. It would be a wonderful balance to our modern science and technology if we could learn their insights. The face in the clouds in the center looks like a female face. Her chalice is in the middle. The ankh rises up from the bottom in the center.

This is the only time I have seen an image quite like this. Once again, I thank the Great Mother for letting me see this place in person and again in symmetry.

PLATE 12 CHAPTER 11

"The Sunflower charioteer".

PLATE 12 CHAPTER 11 is so bright, it is almost blinding. The sunflowers came from my garden. The charioteer in white, is emerging on the top, looking victorious. He reminds me of the African Bushman hero/god image, - the praying mantis. The wheels are at the bottom in white, and the horses also in white, face in opposite directions. They are coming out of the wheels at the bottom. There seems to be the same pattern here as the jaguar seat image, but more abstract. The flowers at the sides appear like the open jaws of wild cats in the previous picture. Perhaps this is the sun king after being rejuvenated in the dark womb of the goddess, and he appears ready to emerge.

Reversed, the horses in blue and yellow are facing outward on either side. There is a chalice chariot, with the mantis image in the center, in the new light coming up from the bottom. At the bottom and the top in green, the scarab or mantis is making his way up through the center, pushing up the sun. I see the wings of the caduceus in yellow near the top. The stem of the caduceus goes down the center. It is like we can see the entire journey of the scarab in the center of this chariot. Just under the wings of the caduceus, I can see the dancers in green and white, dancing him into life.

PLATE 13 CHAPTER 11

The chariot of the Owl and Bat.

PLATE 13 CHAPTER 11 appears to be the chariot of the owl and bat, which represents the death and rebirth aspect of both the feminine and masculine symbolically in nature. I see this combination often in symmetry. This image shows the owl upright and the bat when reversed. Together, they make the six-corner star, which is the yin and yang of nature. The owl image also appears like the Sheela-na-gig goddess, which is the crone aspect of the feminine. Her image is seen above the doorways of old churches and temples throughout Europe.

The dance of life coming into and out of being is very dramatic on both sides upright and reversed. Upright, the dance takes place on either side of her chalice-womb, and the dancers appear to be native women of the first peoples of the Southwest. These dancers are also in the position of being the goddess's hands.

Our hands, along with the heart, are the dancing aspect of the human body. I have heard from both Hawaiian's and Eskimo's that hands are powerful story-tellers in their dances. The Eskimo's even put on gloves when they danced, which were worn interestingly, as protection for those who watched, because of the power the hands carried in them. This picture helps me understand what they might be saying. Perhaps in their storytelling, they are being the hands of the divine feminine. As I have said, the divine feminine often speaks to us through stories.

In reverse, the dancers in white are on both sides of the bats head and neck. The bat wings go out from the top on both sides. The bat image is always seen above the mouth of the masculine principle. The ancients often used dance to represent cosmic creation. It is seen all the time in symmetry. There is a scepter in the middle, which was considered the phallic spirit or the rod of power for the masculine.

PLATE 14 CHAPTER 11

"The dance"

PLATE 14 CHAPTER 11 is one of my favorite images of the dance, which I found on the beach. This is where the dance of the waves is constantly present. It appears like a dance of abandonment or sheer ecstasy. This dance is happening on either side of the womb chalice at the bottom.

I can see a king enthroned here with his scepter. He seems to be wearing a crown or headdress of two doves, which shows the masculine chalice seated within the female womb. The dress of the large dancers has the appearance of dove's wings. Perhaps like the tjet or the "matrix of Isis", the chalice here is holding the diamond holder, the *dorje*. Reversed, we see the feminine counterpart to the *dorje*, the bell where his head was. In the East, they still know what these instruments mean and use them symbolically. This knowledge has been lost in the West.

Near the top, I see a female figure facing inward in the middle with a smile. Her hands on either side seem to be revealing a caduceus. It is a picture that has the appearance of pure joy. I can get this feeling when I am walking on a beautiful beach with a loved one.

Reversed is the pyramid womb with the king, the scarub, and the sun emerging from the top like the ball with wings. As the scarab emerges from the top, it is surrounded by the shape of a butterfly. From this direction, the dancers are now witnessing this beautiful transformation taking place. In the butterfly, it also appears, like the two doves and snakes are facing outward on either side. Inside the top of the pyramid, it appears like his head and her torso are superimposed over each other. This is the womb of transformation.

This picture reminds me of a poem by the abbot, Hildegard of Bingen. She writes of Sophia, wisdom of God "Come to me … I'll strengthen you. Then you can seek the lost coin and give it the crown of joyful perseverance." Virtue replies, "Glorious queen, kindest mediator, we come, dancing!"

PLATE 15 CHAPTER 11

"The dance and the sacrifice".

PLATE 15 CHAPTER 11 is the archetypal dance we see in all the elements. It is the dance that includes the joy of life and the sacrifice of death. Both of these pictures are found in nature's natural symmetry, and they have the same theme. One is found in a snowflake from William Bentley's book <u>Snow Crystals</u> from Dover Press. The other is a reflection of a river in the Cascade Mountains. The snowflake shows a skull-like face with an arrow going up through it. Under the skull at the neck are two dancers who seem to be dancing with abandon. I interpret this to be like the

Sheela-na-gig image of the death aspect of the feminine. She has a skull-like face, and her legs go out on either side. Keep in mind that you are seeing one-sixth of a tiny snowflake, smaller than the eye can see without a magnified lens.

Next to it is the same image but with much more detail. We see the skull-like face, in a pyramid, like a central mountain, and there is an arrow going through the center. Under her chin is fire, or the sun, possibly going down into the void or womb beneath it.

My first impression was that it was a burning bush that is not consumed. It appears to be a cross section where the god is sacrificed. I think of Golgotha, the "place of the skull," where Jesus was crucified, and wonder if this is a picture of the god's sacrificial, death from nature's view-point. The arrow points upward in both pictures, as if there is a resurrection and ascension about to take place. The dancers beneath the skull look much like the ones in the snowflake. This is the place where the god is sacrificed and becomes the seed of new growth and is born again, ascending upwards.

This reminds me of the galactic center represented by the dark part in the center of this picture. This is where all life in our galaxy begins and ends. The arrow of Sagittarius the archer, goes across the abyss of Scorpius in this galactic center, like this picture.

This picture goes even further and shows us Pan and Rhea. These are the two figures in the Greek pantheon who most represent nature. Pan is in the eye, just under the dark void. Perhaps he is playing the music of the spheres on his flute. You can see his goat legs just above Rhea's darkened, veiled face. She sits in the lotus position right under him, and we can see her breasts. Interestingly enough, Pan and Rhea are also both moons of Saturn, and they seem to be surrounded by a Saturn-shaped circle here. Pan also represents the whole world. Saturn in Roman myth was an earth god, and his wife was Rhea. They both represent the death aspect until it becomes a joyous rebirth.

In this picture reversed, we can see the head of a man with the bat above his mouth like the sacrificial god. The eye is now his third eye. It is like they are playing out a ritual that is timeless. I took this picture in the year 1999. I consider that to be the last year of the age of Pisces. Perhaps the sun of the old age of Pisces is being sacrificed here. All this goes on all around us, but we do not see it without the mirror of symmetry.

PLATE 16 CHAPTER 11

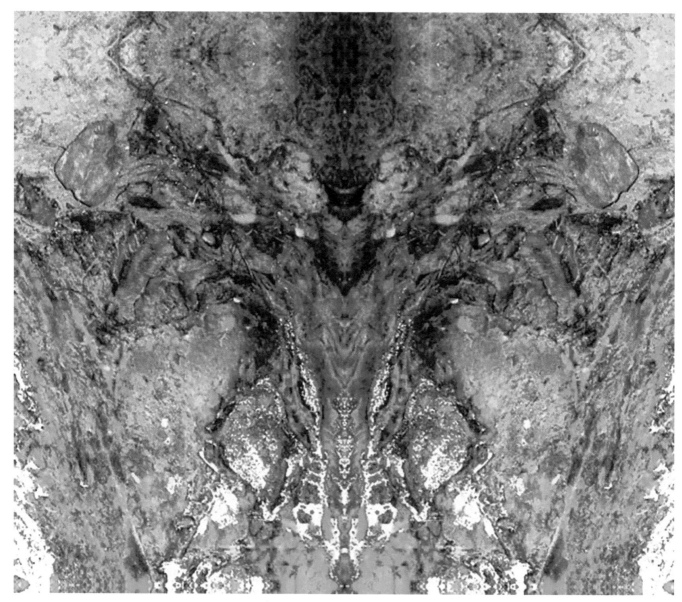

"The womb of a cave by the sea".

PLATE 16 CHAPTER 11 taken in a cave by the sea is the best representation I have depicting the womb of Mother Earth, our chariot. I cannot imagine anything looking more like the beautiful female organs of the primordial divine feminine. On the top on either side of the center, we see highlighted - as only nature can do it—the two doves in bright peach color facing inwards, that always grace the top of the womb or chalice. There are two snakes that are just on top of the doves heads. The whole picture looks like a dance of life.

In the lower third, we see in the center the "diamond holder," which is the *dorje*, representing the masculine phallus within natures womb. It is blue and appears to be studded with diamonds. This is the way nature brings opposites together, with the masculine embedded within the feminine.

Reversed it appears like the phallus penetrating the lotus. The dancers are in peach color at the bottom. There are many elementals gathered around witnessing this scene. It appears as if two light colored horses are facing inwards to witness this. The horse has always been related to the divine feminine.

Looking at this picture, I think of my question to the grade school children of where artists get inspiration for art, I can say with my whole being, "Nature!"

PLATE 17 CHAPTER 11

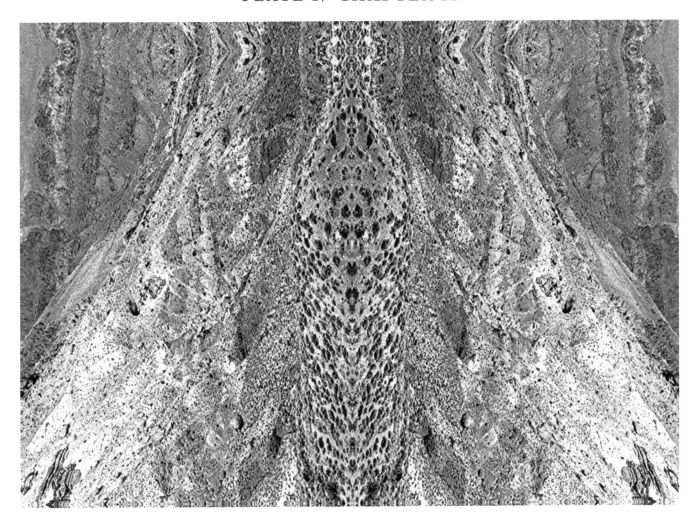

PLATE 17 CHAPTER 11 was taken in what has been called Death Valley by the immigrant culture of this country. The ancients and the first peoples would not have called it by this name. This is a picture of the coming together of opposites which shows her lower body with the masculine herm within. The whole picture has the appearance of a butterfly transformation taking place. It is also a good picture of what the ancient Egyptians called the ankh and the *tjet*. I have cut out the center of this picture taken from plate 17, and outlined what I am seeing for the next plate, 18.

PLATE 18 CHAPTER 11

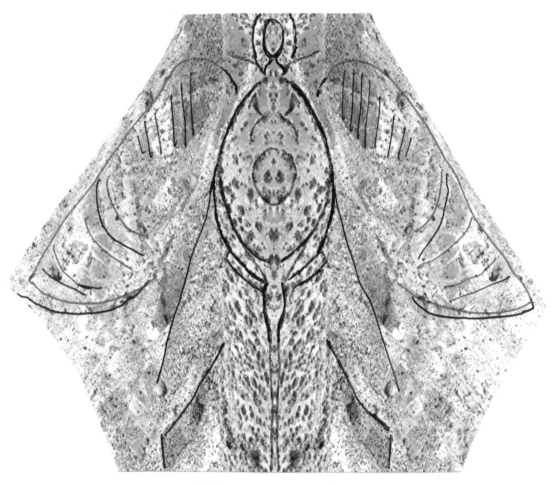

"The tjet, the matrix of Isis"

Barbara Walker, in her book *The Woman's Dictionary of Symbols and Sacred Objects*, describes the tjet as "one of Egypt's most sacred amulets, thought to be an archaic form of the ankh, and apparently resembling a small standing angel." "The Coptic makes it clear that this amulet was intended to represent the vulva or matrix of Isis," Isis being the divine feminine. **PLATE 18 CHAPTER 11** represents this description in living color.

As the matrix of the divine feminine, this amulet was commonly made of red stone, representing the "stuff of life emanating from the Goddess's genitalia." We can see the red stuff of life here too, along with all the colors of the rainbow. It sings life! In the cut-out center, of plate 18 you can see the scarab at the top climbing up and out as if being reborn. The transformation continues, celebrate and honor it.

PLATE 19 CHAPTER 11

"Her body and his head".

Since the theme of her body and his head comes up so often in symmetry, I would like to show you that for the ancients, this yin yang concept was well understood. In **PLATE 19 CHAPTER 11**, we see a shield design from the Solomon Islands. On the top is his head, and just below like a mirror image is her body. I have seen this same theme depicted in many other cultures, placed together like this as mirror images. It makes me wonder how this theme was lost to modern culture.

This is all part of bringing consciousness back into balance. Ask a martial arts person, if they would make aggressive yang actions, without compensating this with the yielding yin actions. They know everything is a balance. This needs to be a part of our way of thinking as well, if we are to be in balance.

One of the most heart-breaking things I have ever seen on TV was watching a group of indigenous peoples of the Amazon forest standing and watching in horror as the section of forest that was home to them was being clear-cut. It was as if their own heart and lungs were being pulled out as they watched what they considered to be madness and a total violation.

This does not even address the animal species that were killed or displaced. This is the evidence of the split of yin–yang values and how they have become imbalanced. Some company made some good money doing this, but the peoples who had lived there for countless generations are now homeless. If these values rule, then all of us are in danger.

CHAPTER 12

Mother of the Enlightened
(In the Hidden Third)

THE SUM TOTAL OF LIFE, body, soul, and spirit begins with the divine feminine as, the deep, the void, the womb, the galactic center, and the prima materia within our depths. The alchemist's job is to find this coarse, unrefined material, project it, re-claim it, and refine it. This includes all the vast elements in our lives, and how they affect us in our daily life, both consciously and unconsciously.

The elements we are unconscious of, we tend to project, until we realize we have to reclaim and become conscious of them within ourselves. Only then can we refine it. This process is not just in relation to our personal selves, but also in relation to the collective we are a part of as well. The issues we have neglected and would rather not address, are the ones that end up in our face to work on.

Birthing consciousness in the collective is brought about by those individuals who are willing to pick up the divine destiny they are given. This allows us to be the mid-wife for the divine mother, and help her birth her divine son, the Enlightened One, in our lives. In this process, we become enlightened.

This birth has been imagined throughout the ages as either a hermaphrodite, born of the "World egg", or as the "divine son born of a Virgin." For the alchemist, it's the Virgin Sophia, wisdom of God, who gives us the fertile heart's and minds with which to give birth to something more whole and healing, turning the base elements in our lives into refined gold, and a wasteland into the abundance of life. Her totem is the dove, which is also the totem of the Holy Spirit. It is also, as we have seen, the dove that is always seen flanking the chalice of all life. This is seen all the time in symmetry. Barbara Walker writes in her book _The Woman's Encyclopedia of Myths and Secrets,_ "She was God's mother, the great revered virgin in whom the Father was concealed from the beginning before he had created anything." Her son is "the savior and begetter of all things, and Sophia is the Mother of all. Every culture had their own name for her."

Many have never heard of Sophia. The first large Christian temple ever built goes back to the sixth century AD and is in Constantinople. It was named - Hagia Sophia, which means "Holy Female Wisdom" in Greek. Amazingly, this temple is still standing today. Later, the church fathers falsely claimed that the name Hagia Sophia really meant "Christ, the Word of God." Then they changed Sophia into a saint, and she was forgotten. All former reference of her was then suppressed. This was the beginning of the patriarchal age of Pisces, when there was an effort to remove all traces of the previous matriarch and the significance of the divine Sophia. Maybe in this new age, it is time to begin to realize consciously the need for the yin yang balance.

135

You might think this is all nonsense in a day and age when we blindly worship rationality, but our rational egos have been likened to a cork bobbing on the surface of a huge ocean, thinking it's in control when vast networks and systems in our bodies and in the universe are at work in and around us, influencing us from the moment we are conceived. The reality is that life is much more than ego rationality.

Imagine what it would be like to have our heads, hearts, bodies, and spirits working together without any fragmentation. This is the reason we must be focused on the center and what I think of as the true "Holy Grail."

In the biblical books of Wisdom literature, there seems to have been a conflict and controversy between those who followed Sophia, and those who followed Yahweh. This was a symptom of the transition from the collective matriarchy, into the patriarchy. It could have been that the old age of the matriarchy and its values had become imbalanced and corrupt, just as the patriarch and its values have become today.

In this information age, we know that information is not enough. Wisdom is what brings meaning and empowerment with purpose to our lives. It is also what gives us the possibility of evolving and solving problems that our ego imbalance has created.

In my process, I have found that often my ego does not even know what to pray for, so I pray for the renewing of my heart and mind. This lets my higher Self know that I am willing to continue the process that brings about the birth of the divine masculine, the Enlightened One within myself. In this way, I give over the reigns, which allows me to live with a sense of a higher purpose.

We have heard about the precious stone worth any price, the philosopher's stone, the holy grail, and the quest to find them, but how many even know how to begin on this quest? Carl Jung reminds us that, "Nature is not matter only, she is also spirit." We have forgotten this as we have allowed our oceans, air, and earth to be trashed. We have forgotten that the womb of Mother Earth is also a sacred Holy Grail, that contains the divine spirit within. We will see in symmetry the divine masculine, the *dorje* (the six-pronged object also called the "diamond holder" that contains the lightning bolt of the divine masculine spirit. This too has largely been forgotten. These are the symbols of the coming together of opposites in balance that is needed for creating and sustaining all life.

If we could see and understand this, we would see the beginning of a new way of perceiving and a new sense of responsibility for contributing to this balance. Then we will all be on the quest of the Holy Grail and the Enlightened One.

Let's look at how Mother Nature and her divine masculine spirit presents this understanding through the mirror of symmetry. Remember, the divine feminine uses symbols and imagery, not words, to show us the truth we fail to see otherwise. She also uses our imaginations, so shut off the rational minds for now, and use your imagination's as you look through natures mirror of life.

PLATE 1 CHAPTER 12

The *dorje*, the bell, and the sixcorner star that symbolized the union of opposites.

In **PLATE 1 CHAPTER 12** we see the sixcorner star of overlapping triangles seen in so many mandalas made by nature's sacred geometry. This star is not just the one in the center but also those in the upper and lower parts of the center as well. The diamond jewel in the center is a symbol of the union of water and fire, male and female, and spirit and matter. This image is pictured contained in the Great Mother's womb as "the deep."

PLATE 1 CHAPTER 12 was taken at the coast, in a tide pool teeming with life. It isn't until I place it in symmetry though that I start to see the full significance. Since the symbol of the *dorje* has been lost to Western culture, let's reintroduce this symbol once again.

Turning this picture on its side, we can see the fiery lightning-bolt effects of this six-pronged "diamond holder," the *dorje*, which is perpetually immersed in the deep watery womb. This image is being displayed here by the (in-between world of the elementals.) This world is normally not seen by our rational ego. This symbol has been used by many esoteric religions as a symbol of enlightenment, and the awakening to consciousness. Becoming conscious is often thought of as a lightningbolt experience.

The *dorje* is used inseparably as a religious tool with the bell. Bells were thought of as the feminine aspect that was the counterpart of the masculine *dorje*. The bell would sound as the lightning bolt struck. Bells are the instrument that has always been used to call us to our highest calling. I can see the bell in this picture on the upright side, with the rounded bottom at the top of the sixcorner star in the top middle. The bell is surrounded by the lightning bolts in this picture. The bell's clapper is the pure white shaft seen hanging down the middle. Many cultures through-out history have considered these symbols sacred, and part of the quest for enlightenment that is from the divine.

Dan Eden, on his web-site, talks about the *dorje* and also prints a prayer in the form of a poem—The Bride" by Saint John of the Cross. I would also like to pass this on to you. This poem describes a person who is on their quest to enlightenment.

"Ah - who can cure me?
Now make an end and yield yourself completely;
I beg you, send me no more messengers from today,
For what I yearn to know, they cannot tell me.

Oh, life, how is it you endure
Not living where your life is - how continue
Since close to death you draw
As you receive each arrow

Begotten of the Loved One deep within you?
Extinguish all my sorrows,
For no other is able to release them,
and let my eyes behold you,
you who are there light,
For you alone do I desire to keep them.

PLATE 2 CHAPTER 12

"In the deep".

PLATE 2 CHAPTER 12 is another picture of a tide pool on the coast. We have within this womb of the deep" a large white diamond. The diamond was considered the stone of the Goddess. Superimposed over it is the (HAVH) that we see in the center of the wheel of time, like the Mayan calendar. This is a timeless yin yang image. In this picture, the lightning seems to be coming into the center on the sides in yellow. Every way you look at this picture it appears to be a diamond holder within the womb of the deep.

PLATE 3 CHAPTER 12

"The dorje".

PLATE 3 CHAPTER 12 appears like a huge *dorje*. This image too looks as if it is completely studded with diamonds. I can also see a caduceus, with the snakes coming together at the top in a heart shape here as well. (A) is at the top and (V)at the bottom, but they also intersect in the middle. The (H) is in the center horizontally. There is an X in the center as well, and it is hooked. This hooked cross is another symbol, the meaning of which has been lost but is being studied again today. I see it in symmetry all the time. This could represent the rune of partnership. There is no upside down to the (X)symbol. It is (A) and (V) in balance. From it flows all life.

If we look at just the top half of the picture, we can also see the image of the square and the compass which is used in Freemasonry weather it is comprehended or not. Some Freemasons put a letter G in the center to represent God. God is not always spelled with the letter G in other cultures though. I do see however a royal king like figure with a jewel studded crown in the center of this square and compass. It is in the superimposed V over the letter A which is very similar in appearance. Perhaps the king represents the God. In the center horizontally we have the (X) with what appears like what could be the lightning bolts on the four sides.

PLATE 4 CHAPTER 12

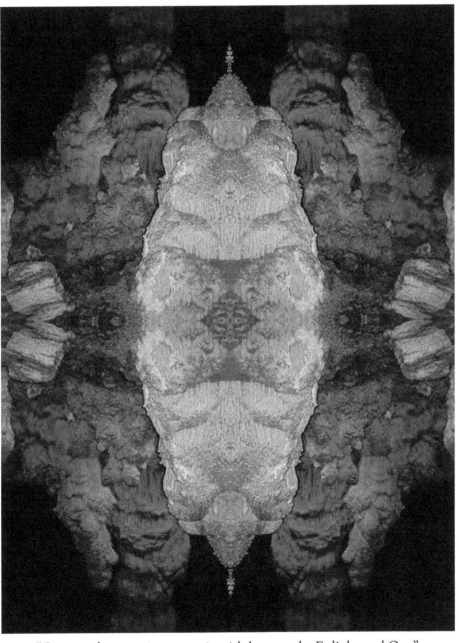

"Cave mother as prima materia with her son the Enlightened One".

PLATE 4 CHAPTER 12 is from a picture I took in a cave, another symbol of the divine womb of our Mother Earth. Not surprisingly, we find the Great Mother here as the lumpy coarse rock of prima materia." She appears to be proudly showing us her son, the enlightened one, seated on her lap. Her lap is also a chariot with the axle of the wheels on either side of the middle. We can see the four-fold snake symbol in brown at the very center, which also symbolizes the chariot.

Like many images of the goddess, she appears with four arms and hands, telling us she is the mother of the four elements of earth, water, fire, and air. All the elements appear to be represented here. She is the earth, the water in blue trickles down in a four-fold spiral around him, and the fire glows in the center. Perhaps the element of air is the transcendent element of this picture. I see a butterfly image in the center that he is sitting on. Perhaps this butterfly represents the air element to finally bring about the four-fold transformation.

PLATE 5 CHAPTER 12

"A close-up of her son".

From the same picture, cropped in half, is a close-up of her son, the Enlightened One. He sits in the lotus position, with the chariot beneath him. If we look at him closely, we can see that he is a hermaphrodite, and it is as if he has just emerged from the world egg in front of him, on his lap. He looks like the image of a divine being the ancients called Phanes or Eros. He was also known as the Aion, emerging from the cosmic egg of time into a new age. He was described as entwined with a serpent. He wore a helmet and had golden wings.

This hermaphrodite here also wears a helmet and has golden wings. His helmet has a flame on the top. This kind of helmet with a flame is called a Ushnisha, which is a helmet worn by the Enlightened Ones, and it was a sign of divine intelligence. This headdress shows his spiritual power. Another version of this is the halo or aureole that is seen on the heads of the Enlightened Ones as well. This Enlightened One is the one who has succeeded in drawing spiritual energy up through his body to the top of the head.

Barbara Walker tells us that Eastern mystics associated this with the immortal soul that they said was "made of the same ethereal light as the stars, which came down from heaven to inhabit the body of the flesh, and then return to the starry heaven after death. Like the prophet Elijah in the Bible, this is the way of the Enlightened One. He brings opposites together, by bringing the heavens down into the depths, and then returns to the heavens.

Like the Aion, he is emerging from the egg at the beginning of this new age. He was considered the "firstborn of God", and the light that emerges from the darkness of the womb of the abyss or the primal Mother. Plato called this hermaphrodite the first-born Eros, the oldest of the deities who was another charioteer who gave souls the strength to ascend to heaven after death.

He also reminds me of the little Buddha like figure we see cropping up in mathematical fractal images, spontaneously reoccurring at intervals. This fractal image is called the "Mandelbrot set," which is also found in a mathematically symmetrical setting with an axis upon which it is surrounded. Perhaps he would be what the physicist might call the "God particle."

Jung describes this as a "psychoid archetype," meaning he is not purely physical, yet not purely psychic either. He is in the "in-between", but definitely there. This is why the work of the alchemist is so allusive, yet inclusive, and holistic. It is both a spiritual and a psychological path. He is much more than logical, rational, and concrete.

This figure wears a golden heart diadem that is within the star around his neck. The top of the star is also, his mother's lips. Her eyes are in the red rock on either side of his head. As I look, I can almost see her wink, like she is showing me her prize. For sure, she is showing me a mystery that I can only hope to eventually understand through my experiences.

PLATE 6 CHAPTER 12

"With her primordial world egg".

PLATE 6 CHAPTER 12 is another picture of the mother as "the deep" holding the world egg. This egg seems to be teeming with life. Within this egg at the bottom half, we can make out a small version of the charioteer, as if emerging from the egg. The wheels are beneath him and we can see the horse's heads in blue going in opposite directions. It is a very primal picture, that never-the-less shows the potential for the abundance of life. The charioteer appears to be seated on her lap.

Reversed, I see the head of a frog at the bottom of the picture, which is one of the most primitive totem images of the goddess, showing us, this is a primal state. It seems to be bringing together the waters of the deep, with the fire beneath it.

She appears to be the Mother of creatures also, because I can see the heads of many different creatures on either side of her. They say that all life at one time came from the sea.

PLATE 7 CHAPTER 12

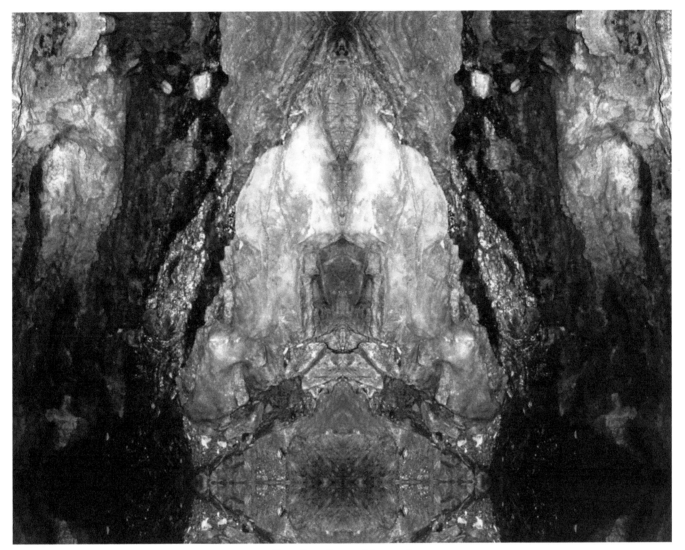

"On his throne/chariot".

PLATE 7 CHAPTER 12 is another cave image of the Enlightened One. He too sits in the lotus position. His throne is graced by two peacock's on either side, facing out. Peacocks are considered sacred to the divine feminine interestingly enough, as the "Queen of Heaven." His chariot appears as if it is covered with stars. Again, it is like the starry heavens are drawn down into the depths of the earth. The starry heavens were in the imagination of the ancients, like the peacock's tail with its eyes, which represented the all-seeing Eye Mother of wisdom and justice.

He also wears a golden halo and a crown on his head. Above his head is the top of an ankh, with its stem going down through his face. I have seen many Egyptian pictures of Isis, the divine feminine, giving an ankh to the god, as if giving him life. The ankh had two meanings: both life, and as a hand mirror. This is a coming together of the opposites in the mirror reflection of symmetry within the feminine. The depths are being mirrored by the heavens.

There appears to be two glowing beings around his neck, as if they are attending him. When I look closely at them, I see they could be dancing. The dance is also related to the heart, which is the organ in our bodies that is in a perpetual dance. They seem to be surrounding his heart.

His face appears like the chrysalis of a butterfly. The chrysalis is the third stage of the four-fold development of the butterfly. Perhaps these glowing white beings represent the cocoon phase of his life. There may be a transformation taking place, and we are witnessing something in progress. The fourth stage, - the butterfly of transformation is yet to be.

When we look at the peacocks from the opposite direction, facing inward, they become cherubs with wings and a white headdress. These cherubs seem to be gazing above his head, as if they are witnessing something or anticipating something that is about to happen.

I see him as if meditating on the Holy Grail in front of him. This is what the charioteer in the Tarot deck is said to be meditating on, before his chariot starts to move. Perhaps this is what he does just before his incarnation begins.

There is one thing that surprises me here, and that is the two horses on either side of his throne/chariot near the bottom. Usually, as we have seen, these horses face outward and pull in opposite directions, but in this instance, the horses face inward toward the center. We saw this also in the womb image by the coast. It is as if they too face the center and await the moment of transformation that will take them forward. Perhaps this is the enlightened charioteer who is becoming totally aligned with his star of destiny. The star is in front of the grail in the center as superimposed triangles. He appears to be totally in his center. The word for this picture is "Om".

I sense that it may have something to do with the crowned being in the sanctuary-like enclosure at his stomach. It appears to represent the feminine principle. Perhaps this sanctuary is like the alchemist's furnace, which is also a vessel representing the feminine principle in alchemy. It is also called the vessel of Hermes the hermaphrodite and the dwelling place of the anima mundi or the temple of the world soul. The purpose for the use of this vessel was to "dissolve the present, and reconstitute the future." What a good description this is of the cocoon phase of transformation! This is the process our egos must go through in our own transition from our lumpy lives, to a purer and more transformed vessel for the world soul to dwell. Under this, we have the chalice with the herm in its center as a coming together of opposites that brings about this transformation.

When I see these side figures, I look at what directions they are facing. Just like magnets and electricity, with their positive and negative force, these figures on the sides looking into the center are facing the masculine principle, and those looking away from the center are attending the feminine principle. There are many overlaps and double-faced images, and it confirms that these images are androgynous by nature. They help me understand and identify what I am looking at.

Above the sanctuary-like image, we see what looks like the winged top of a caduceus, for the coming together of opposites in a healing way. Hermes was the Greek god who carried the caduceus. He is the hermaphrodite who brings together the archetypes of Hermes, and Aphrodite. This is how nature works, whether it be life, birth, transformation, healing, or electricity. Nothing happens without the coming together of opposites in some way. With this coming together, transformation can take place, life can begin, and balance can be restored. This is why the divine feminine can-not be neglected. Reversed we see the double snake caduceus top in the form of a huge heart.

I found this Enlightened One's feet to be interesting near the center, close to the bottom. They have a double appearance, both as shoes, and in another way as two fish. Pisces rules the feet, so perhaps, this is what is represented here. Perhaps this is the transformational phase between the ages. Another way of thinking about it is that fish are a species that is not fully evolved. His arms look like snakes. I found an alchemical picture that helped me to understand this image better. Alchemy is not a nonsense science, it was a sacred science. It had to endure the inquisition, so it was obscured to remain under the radar of their dogmatic age. Carl Jung is the most recent person to seriously study this science. Let's look at the alchemist's rendition of this image.

PLATE 8 CHAPTER 12

Figure 10.7
The Pandora picture: "A mirror Image of the Holy Trinity."
"The Pandora picture".

PLATE 8 CHAPTER 12 shows an alchemical picture that has been called, "The Pandora picture." It is also, interestingly enough, called "A Mirror Image of the Holy Trinity." Both Carl Jung and Edward Edinger as well as others who have delved into alchemy, have talked about this picture in length. It is a Christian theme, with an alchemical process dropped into it.

This image is portraying the transformation of the all-masculine Christian trinity into a quaternary that includes the divine feminine as Mary, who is being received into heaven in her bodily form, and being coronated as queen of heaven. Jung was excited by this church dogma when it was introduced in 1950. He thought it represented the feminine principle, which also represents material life, and the role of the ego in relation to the Self. He thought that the feminine principle had been left out of the all-masculine Christian trinity, so this was what was needed for the balance and healing to take place at the end of this patriarchal age of Pisces.

This Pandora picture is divided into upper and lower halves that look very different, but in -fact, they are supposed to be mirroring each other somehow, and they are happening simultaneously. Neither could happen without the other taking place at the same time. It's another version of the heavens being reflected in the depths.

In the upper half, we see Mary being coronated as the queen of heaven in a totally positive situation. With her in heaven is the Father and the Son and the Holy Spirit in the form of a dove. The lower half of the picture however, is a totally different kind of situation. We see a shield-like container, where a haloed figure is pulling another haloed figure out of a lumpy rock. He has snake-like arms and fish-like feet. This is what made me think of this picture in relation to the previous one.

This is not representing something intellectual; it is experiential, and it represents an experience that for the transforming ego, is a real ordeal but necessary for the process. It has been described as "the extraction of Mercurius out of Prima Materia." Mercury is the same archetype as Hermes. It is also related to the anima mundi, the feminine force of the universe that is diffused throughout all nature, according to Plato. Jung and Edinger call this the being that is being freed from the shackles of matter, and the son of the great world. Like Hermes, Mercury has a double nature that is both female and male, bad and good, poison and its antidote. Like Sophia, he can unite all, and he connects the heavens to the underworld.

Here, we have a paradoxical but uniting relationship with the heavens reflecting the depths simultaneously, and in some mysterious way, they are mirroring each other. Like the opposites coming together, one is celebrating something very positive in heaven, while the other is going through a real ordeal in the very depths.

I had to wonder what this picture meant to me. It was definitely describing a mystery. Here again, as a charioteer, I knew I did not hold the reigns. Ego-hood in this incarnation is definitely having to deal with the ordeal's life presents us. There are times when we feel like we are trapped, and other times when we feel like we are in a cocoon, waiting for the time of emergence, not knowing what will be emerging when the transformation unfolds. This is a time of letting go and purging when you can't explain to friends and family what is going on in your life, and why you seem to be so out of it. This is the dissolving process, so that there can be a reemergence in a transformed way. As your ego feels like you have completely dropped out, it may look this way to others around you too. There are no explanations that can be given, to justify yourself.

This is the way I felt, when I started to go through a series of situations that took me down into my depths. I went through breast cancer, chemotherapy, and radiation treatment. At the same time, I was taking care of my husband, who had a severe stroke the year before, and was left severely crippled. People sympathized with the outward ordeal I was going through, but what they did not know was, that an even bigger ordeal was happening to me inwardly. In a way, it was easier for me to go through this dropout experience, without people wondering what my problem was. They just accepted the outward situation as the full reason for my drop-out time.

Then I had a symbolic symmetrical experience. Living symbolically, as I have said, is important to this work. It allows you to observe yourself from a more protected vantage point rather than just in hard mundane reality. It allows you to be a witness of your life in a more objective and loving way.

I had ordered some special tea on-line to lift my spirits. I love the British saying, "Keep calm and carry on." I have a cup with this saying on it. I got my package in the mail and opened it, only to find that they had sent me the wrong tea! They explained that they no longer carried the tea I had ordered, but that they had sent me a tea that was almost identical to it, and they thought I would like it just as well. I was disappointed until I saw the name of this tea that they had sent me, to replace the one I had ordered. The tea was called "Queen's Coronation Tea." Tears came into my eyes because I understood in that moment what this picture was telling me.

I knew then, amazingly enough, that these two totally different situations were coming together and reflecting each other at that moment in my life. It gave me the sense that I was part of a purposeful process. The one could not happen without the other, so I was doing the work and fulfilling this process. I was picking up the star, and doing my part. The heavens were being reflected and in my depths at the same time. This is how the higher Self gives meaning to our life. It may sound strange, but a meaningful ordeal is so much easier to deal with than a meaningless ordeal, where there is no consciousness happening.

I fixed myself some "Queen's Coronation Tea" and poured it into my "Keep calm and carry on" cup and celebrated the process that can bring enlightenment. One morning I woke with a poem in my head. I think it was from Sophia.

In your depths,
you can mirror the heavens.
What are these depths?
These depths are the waters of life.

PLATE 9 CHAPTER 12

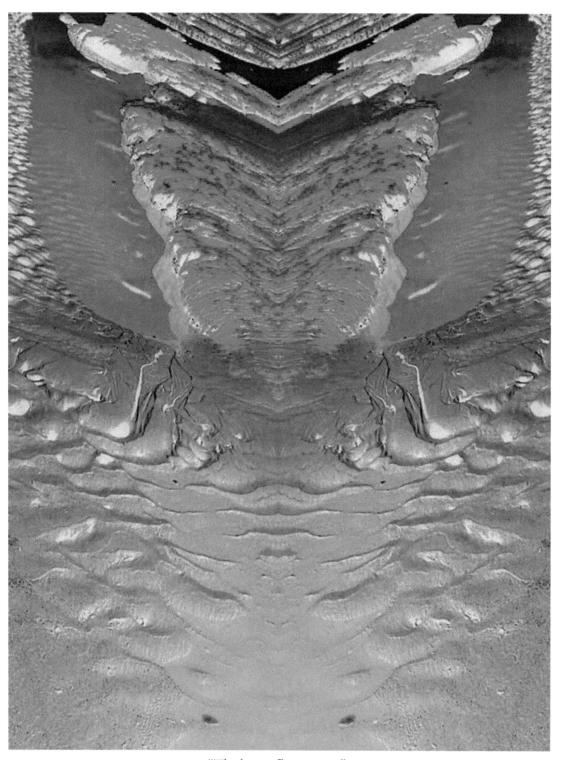

"The butterfly emerges".

PLATE 9 CHAPTER 12 dramatically shows the Enlightened One emerging as the beautiful transformed butterfly. The butterfly now becomes his head this time instead of the chrysalis in the previous picture. The figures facing inward by his neck appear as if they are paying homage to the miracle they have just witnessed. When I was working with this picture, I decided to reverse the colors to make it appear even more like a transformation of opposites coming together.

PLATE 10 CHAPTER 12

"The eye of wonder".

Mother Earth may be brown, black, red, or green, but her eyes are blue. Here again, within the depths of a cave, the mother's womb, we see "the stone of the hermaphrodite" or the philosopher's stone, which symbolized the marriage of heaven and earth, spirit and matter.

Alchemists had a secret with occult significance that went like this— "Visit the interior of the earth. By purification, you will find the hidden Stone." This is the substance of universal creation that transforms matter from the base to the refined. This stone was not a stone at all, it was a coming together of the elements going from lumpy chaos to the transforming, purified balance of these same elements. When they come together in this way, they are able to reveal what is truly sacred—the Mother of all and her Divine Son.

Here in the center of **PLATE 10 CHAPTER 12** is the eye that I would liken perhaps to the eye of the cervix within the womb of the mother. It is said that the hermaphrodite is born of two mountains. In the whites of this eye, in this womb image, I can see the two mountains. Lapis lazuli traditionally symbolized the primal element of all life - water. Barbara Walker tells us that the Egyptians used to bury lapis amulets with the mummies in place of their heart to bring about regeneration in the afterworld. The lapis is in the heart of this picture.

Lapis lazuli was also known as the "stone of truth" that was sacred to the goddess, as the "All-seeing eye," Ma'at. African pygmies still know Ma'at as the goddess of truth and justice, and as "the womb" as well. It was said that "the gods themselves were constrained to live by Ma'at's laws." The sun god was told that "the goddess Ma'at "embraceth thee both at morning and at evening." Her womb was the sun boat that carried the old weakened sun back into herself at night and then gave birth to the rejuvenated sun in the morning. This could be true of the end of a sun's age and the beginning of another sun's age as well. Like the sun boat with the stone of truth in the center, there is work being done at the beginning of this new age.

This alchemical eye symbol also appears like a bit of the blue heavens descended into the depths of earth. Like the "eye of Ma'at", it looks upward into the heavens. The alchemist J. Bohme describes it as "eternity's eye of wonder," that reveals itself in the mirror of wisdom Sophia, the all-seeing Mother. Bohme also said, "No knowledge can be gained with the corporeal eyes, but with the eyes in which life gives birth to itself in me."

I begin to sense what he was talking about when I see this picture. He referred to it as "seeing through the ground, "from above and outside nature." This can only be seen in the hidden third of symmetry and through our mirrored life experiences, as one is working to become conscious. Because it is normally hidden from us, it is able to avoid ego tampering, and yet in time, it emerges into newness of life. This is how divine wisdom reveals itself to us. This is why it remains a mystery.

Joseph Campbell, in his series of talks with Bill Moyer, mentions that it was the paradoxical "neutral angels, that brought this "stone" down to earth." These were the angels who did not take part in the war in heaven. Perhaps we can see some of these neutral angels in these pictures too. They are the ones found in attendance on either side of the hidden third of symmetry. They seem to be doing their work and doing it well, but we do not see them with our corporeal eyes. We only see them through the mirror of symmetry.

Mother Nature gives us wisdom when we observe and attend her closely. A good example of this is watching the caterpillar go through its amazing transformation into a butterfly. It is a great encouragement, knowing that such a transformation is possible. If it can happen to the butterfly, it could happen to us too. The more we observe and participate with faith, the more we learn, and the more we open ourselves to the possibility of this transformation.

This is why I am so concerned for the younger generation of children who do not even reference for Mother Nature. They will be getting vertical reality instead of wisdom, unless we can help them make this transition, and re-introduce them to their Mother Nature, so they too can experience this "Eye of Wonder" for themselves.

PLATE 11 CHAPTER 12

"The void".

PLATE 11 CHAPTER 12 shows the Great Mother as "the void", which is also the womb. Like the Sheela-na-gig aspect of the goddess, she is showing us in this picture, the void from which we came and to where we will go. Her hands are at the top of the void on either side. It also appears like this void also belongs to the "Mother of Creatures." I can see a diversity of creatures all around her. There are two creatures in particular that stand out, both in blue. The goddess as the dark void is at the gate of the underworld, and she was always accompanied by two dogs. I can see the dogs heads just under her golden hands. It was thought that the dogs carried the dead back to the mother through this dark void.

I also see what appears like perched blue jays on either side under the dogs' heads. The blue jay has a paradoxical reputation like that of the hermaphrodite. Ted Andrews, in his book *"Animal Speak,"* mentions that "in Greek mythology, the union of Mother Earth Gaea and Father Heaven Uranus resulted in the first creatures." This is what this picture appears like to me. Interestingly, the jay comes from the Latin word *Gaia* or *Gaea*, which is also the name given to Mother Earth. This, as Andrews mentions, shows the blue jay's "ability to link the heavens and the earth to access each for greater power." This is very much like the role we see played by Hermes, who could go up to the heavens, and down into the underworld. He also brought male and female together as the hermaphrodite.

As this blue jay stares into the abyss, he is fearless. This makes him a powerful survivor. There is the element of the wild in him, but also of mastery. Like the horses of the charioteer, he can go in either direction. We are warned to stay in our center though, because he is also a trickster.

The wild aspect of the mother of creatures is another thing that our culture has lost respect for in our modern values. This is to our detriment. Our culture was the one that chose cattle over the mighty buffalo. It was the buffalo that once ruled the plains, and fed and clothed all the people. They did not need to be tended or fed, and they had a strength and air about them that far surpassed the cattle of today.

Unless we can learn to make room for the wild parts of nature in ourselves, our quest will never have a chance. As in all these images, it is about balance, keeping our focus on the center. We lose something very precious in the balance when we leave out the wild. Just above the void, we can see the hermaphrodite in the lotus position. Perhaps he is emerging from the abyss. On the top in white, we see the scarab emerging with a caduceus. We see the enlightened one again reversed in the center.

PLATE 12 CHAPTER 12

"Coatlicue and Quetzalcoatl".

PLATE 12 CHAPTER 12 reminds me of the Aztec enlightened savior god Quetzalcoatl. He was portrayed in a few different ways. His two aspects represent both creation and destruction. One was as the plumed serpent, covered with feathers, the other as a warrior, who appears in human form with a tall cone-shaped cap and a pendant known as the "wind jewel," which symbolized his movement like the wind. This information came from Barbara Walker's book _The Woman's Encyclopedia of Myths and Secrets_.

Quetzalcoatl was a divine son born of a virgin. His mother was the virgin goddess "Coatlicue". The Spanish conquistadors were surprised at how many parallels there were between their mythic stories and the Spaniards' stories of Jesus. Both gave their blood for their people and died with the promise of returning someday to save humanity.

Quetzalcoatl had two faces; both seem to appear in this image. Right side up, he reminds me of the feathered snake. He stands here as if wearing a glorious robe made of feathers. His face seems to be coming out of the mouth of a snake, like pictures I have seen of Quetzalcoatl. I see what could be his "wind jewel necklace" that he wore, showing his spiritual power. Under this there appears the scarab pushing upward.

Reversed, he wears the apex hat and appears like he is erupting from a volcano. Perhaps this is his destroyer aspect. His mother, Coatlicue, was the goddess of volcanoe's, so this could be the way he was born out of the depths. In the center, his necklace makes the downward pointing triangle, and reversed, his cone shaped hat makes the upward pointing triangle. Together, they make up the six-corner star right in the center.

All these archetypes are dualistic by nature, as is all life. Carl Jung considered Christ to be an incomplete archetype because he was all good. He suggested that the Anti-Christ might represent the negative side of Christ. Like the fish of the Pisces age, they swim in opposite directions. This is the split that needs to be healed before we can start to become whole.

Some say the same of the Virgin Mary. She too only represents the pure. She also represents the sign of Virgo, the opposing sign of Pisces. Both the masculine and feminine principles need to be made whole and balanced. All the Pisces optimism and idealism has not been able to accomplish this. The elements of our lives need to be brought together in a healing way. Spirit and matter, mind and body need to be joined as one.

I feel our current collective situation can only be transformed by the help of divine intervention, with the cooperation of the willing human ego. The problems we face today are too great and too complex for ego-motivated solutions alone. We need to attend a higher wisdom that can renew our minds and hearts, and put us back in our center.

Our egos need to voluntarily enter the cocoon if we are to emerge transformed. If this happens, the way will be made for us to live the destiny we were meant to live as individuals and as a collective.

Butterflies have been a symbol of human souls searching for a new incarnation. Nature gives us these examples like the caterpillar and the butterfly for us to be able to imagine that there can be a transformative experience that can lead to a whole new beginning.

Do not give up the quest. Humanity really needs to make a leap in evolution at this time. With help from the divine and the willing charioteers poised to begin their work, we can begin a whole new era in human evolution. At this, the beginning of a new age, we too can become the Enlightened Ones.

CHAPTER 13

Conclusion

*"It is true that neither the ancient wisdoms nor the modern sciences are complete
in themselves. They do not stand alone. They call for one another.'*
— *Thomas Merton*

I N THE CHINESE <u>BOOK OF CHANGES</u>—The I-Ching, there are a total of sixty-four hexagrams that are chosen by divination to give guidance and wisdom to our human experiences. These hexagrams can serve to confirm, admonish, or caution us about the possible direction we need to take. It is a way of addressing the oracle.

When I first became aware of the I-<u>Ching</u> at the age of twenty-eight, I had a dream in which a man appeared in front of me, holding up a symbol for me to see. It was not too long before he became frustrated because he realized that not only did I not know what it meant, but also, I didn't even know what it was. He gave me a disgusted look and walked away. This dream startled me, and I wondered what it meant.

About four months later, a friend of mine introduced me to the I-Ching. The first thing I did was look up the symbol I was shown in my dream. It was hexagram #20, "contemplation." According to the <u>"Wilhelm–Baynes edition of the I-Ching,</u> it says, "When things are great, one can contemplate them." Ever since then, the I-Ching has been a source of contemplation and discernment for me throughout my adult life.

This experience caused me to contemplate for the first time the line of communication that was being opened by my unconscious counterpart, (my animus). In Jungian psychology, we have an unconscious counterpart to our ego in our psyche that is only communicated through our dream life, and through active imagination. Before this dream, I did not know my unconscious wanted to communicate with me. My unconscious wanted to be a part of my psychological and spiritual development and be a potential source of understanding in my life. This was the point at which I first started to become symmetrical. I now had a way of mirroring my process on my individual path to wholeness.

Part of this mirroring has been to consult the I-Ching when there were issues great enough to seek wisdom. The waters of life are found in the unconscious, and we need to become aware of this living source in order to tap into it. By doing so, I became aware of this autonomous, timeless, and universal source that Jung called the collective unconscious.

This hexagram "contemplation" has a double meaning, as most of these hexagrams do. It also means being seen and being an example. It is an "I see you, and you see me" kind of experience. In fact, I believe it is necessary for us to have this kind of experience if we are to truly know ourselves. With the help of this hexagram, I could experience consciously, my relationship with my unconscious for the first time. It is also a way of asking for guidance from our higher self. It is a way to attend wisdom, and when you do, you can become an example for others.

We need to contemplate the divine meaning of the important experiences of our lives, not just live them unconsciously. The I-Ching is a good way to seek wisdom beyond our egos and learn to give it expression. This is a time in history for serious contemplation and self-reflection. We need to look into the mirror of symmetry in order to learn to live in a healthy and balanced way.

We are beginning this new age of Aquarius, which is the sign of the water barrier. Learning about the waters of life within ourselves would help us a great deal in the process of making this transition. There is a water barrier in the Tarot deck as well, hexagram XVII: "The Star." The key words for this card are *"inspiration, crystallization, self-recognition, radiating, clear vision, trust in the Self,* and *connection to universal intelligence."* from Gerd Ziegler's <u>Tarot: Mirror of the Soul</u>.

We are in a time of testing. We are being shown the old patterns and ways that no longer work for us. In Alcoholics Anonymous, they call it "stinkin' thinkin'." We need to let go of these old patterns and attend the wisdom of all the ages to make this crossing into this new age.

The second to last hexagram in the I-Ching is called interestingly enough, "after completion." This implies that the transition from the old age to the new is already accomplished. It's now a matter of the details of owning this completion. We know that the devil is in the details, so brace yourself for some hard work. This hexagram tells us it is not a time to go on auto-pilot. If we do not trouble with the details, it can result in indifference, which is a good way to self-sabotage ourselves. We need to be vigilant and learn to discern as well as do our work. Birthing consciousness is hard work. Creativity is hard work, and it is up to us to co-create as we learn our lessons.

Remember too that the stress of this transition is very real, and it affects all of us, especially our children. We need to put positive, encouraging energy out there for them. There is no going backward, so we help one another move forward. Being in nature and communicating positively with nature is another way to help us make this transition. Our children need to know they are part of nature. Nature is their Great Mother on this planet.

The very last hexagram in the I-Ching, is #64, paradoxically enough, called - "before completion." Logically, we would think these two hexagrams would be switched, but we must remember that wisdom is not always according to our logic. There is work ahead because in this in-between time of transition, we must go from disorder and chaos, into a new creative beginning with new potentials. We do not know the quantum leaps we may be asked to make. On this precarious path, it helps to have your way confirmed by wisdom.

The image given for this last hexagram is likened to the stormy and precarious transition from winter and spring into the abundance of summer. Though the conditions are difficult and the task is great, there is the promise of success in this process that can unite diverse and even conflicting forces, bringing them together in harmony and abundance. We are told here that in the time "before completion," success is attained in the "yielding middle." This is much like the way of the charioteer, who must stay in the heart center. This yielding middle line is the feminine principle. This allows the masculine and feminine to come together in harmony. Since it is the heartcenter, there is a right attitude for claiming this completion.

There is another image used in this hexagram to help us make success possible. It's the "way of the old fox" walking over ice in-between seasons. This is the wise and wily fox with plenty of life experience behind him. The young and energetic but naive fox, eager to go for it, needs to be careful and observe older wisdom here. The old fox treads lightly, and carefully, listening for cracks in the ice that could mean disaster. The old fox knows how to choose the safest way to make this precarious crossing. Discernment is more important here than enthusiasm.

This is also an admonishment to the wise old foxes of the world. We need your wisdom at this time. We can't possibly make the younger generation go through this alone. We need to step up and contribute what we know in our hearts and have learned through our experiences.

There is a wonderful quote from Sir Krishna:
"When goodness grows weak,
when evil waxes mighty,

I make for myself a vehicle.
In every age, I return
To deliver the holy,
To destroy the fault of the evildoers,
To establish true goodness."

What is this vehicle? This is the divine feminine working through humanity as willing partners doing the "great work" and being her hands. This vehicle is the individuals who are willing to see and contain within themselves the stress and tension of the opposites of symmetry within-themselves and their society. They know how to go into their yielding center, where the birth of something greater can be experienced.

When your compass tells you something is true and you are living a North Star experience, don't let go of it because others around you do not understand. Some of these experiences, you may not be able to share with others. You might not even be able to put it into words at first. This is when consulting old wisdom like the I-Ching or the Tarot can help you sort out, confront, inform, and confirm the process you are going through. Remember, your ego does not know the way. When you are in a cocoon stage of transformation, this might be the only way to get what you need to sustain yourself. It can inform you without putting you in the spotlight, where the gestation can't take place. Protect yourself from people who would judge you with their egos. The divine feminine is good at protecting her own.

I saw an amazing sight while watching Hurricane Irma on the weather channel. The weather-man observed and pointed out that the eye of the hurricane had taken on the shape of a heart, and it was completely filled with birds. These birds were being protected in this heart-shaped eye. As long as they were in this eye, they were safe. The catch was that they would be dropped off in a totally different place from where they had been caught up. It is a good example of the kind of protection we can have in the storms ahead for us. If you remain in that yielding heart-center, you will make it. Just remember that you may be dropped off in a totally different place. This is another reason our egos need to be focused on the heart center.

Making a mandala is another great way to work on your process. Mandalas are symbols of wholeness, and they can help you in your process of becoming whole. As you make your mandala, use the symbols that come to you, and put them down as if you are doing your work, not just an art project. If you want to make an art project of it as well, fine, but it is second to the process of doing your work.

Don't be overwhelmed by the darkness happening in the world. Limit the chaotic TV time and things that raise your stress level. Work on yourself and be mindful of your motives. You will see you are not perfect, but in the process, you will become like the wise old fox. We need to take every opportunity presented to us to learn and grow. We need to answer the knocks at our door and go where these knocks lead us. We also need to reach out and encourage one another in their process.

There is no telling down the road what will be assigned to us after years of learning. This book was an assignment for me. I would have never predicted the process this book has taken me through. Truly, it felt like I was carrying the star on my back. Now that it is done, it is not something my ego can take the credit for. It was the result of what I have learned through my process as a servant of my higher Self and attending wisdom.

It all starts with the nitty-gritty prima materia that can make our lives so difficult. With the help of the scarab, pushing up consciousness, you become the charioteer, aligned with your destiny. Keep in mind that the charioteer does not hold the reins, so you need to stay in your center, in order-to carry out your true destiny. It is yours alone to share with the divine Self. This is how we must take responsibility and grow as individuals and as a human race. This transition is demanding us to give up our childish, "it's all about me" ways.

In Jung's book *Psychology and Alchemy*, he writes, "It is, of course, impossible to free oneself from one's childhood, without devoting a great deal of work to it". "Nor can it be achieved through intellectual knowledge only; what is alone effective is a remembering that is also a re-experiencing."

Sophia is willing to be there for us to help us in this process. She knows it can be frightening and painful. As a wise mother of the adult children of the world, she can help you in the process of re-parenting, and re-imagining your life. She confirms your process in loving and synchronistic ways. She knows how to unite the fragments of our lives so the healing process can begin. We can no longer be half-people trying to shake off the past. It's time for owning, forgiving, and healing on this quest for wholeness, both personally and collectively.

How many of us have had to face our religious, family, and cultural dysfunction, with it's patterns of abuse and imbalance? We can no longer passively accept these patterns of dysfunction, or we hand our children over to them. We need to live what has been tried in the fire and crucible of our own hearts and lives. It's not about what we have been indoctrinated to believe, it's what we have walked through and learned from our own life experience that matters.

We can no longer project outside of ourselves what we do not want to see in ourselves. Many collective values are not life sustaining, and when they aren't, we need to call them out. We need to listen to people on the front lines of these important issues and support them. Only then can we pass on an inheritance to the next generation that is going to be healing and sustaining. We have to do what we can to make it a much cleaner slate for the next generation to begin their journey. What a gift that would be!

PLATE 1 CHAPTER 13

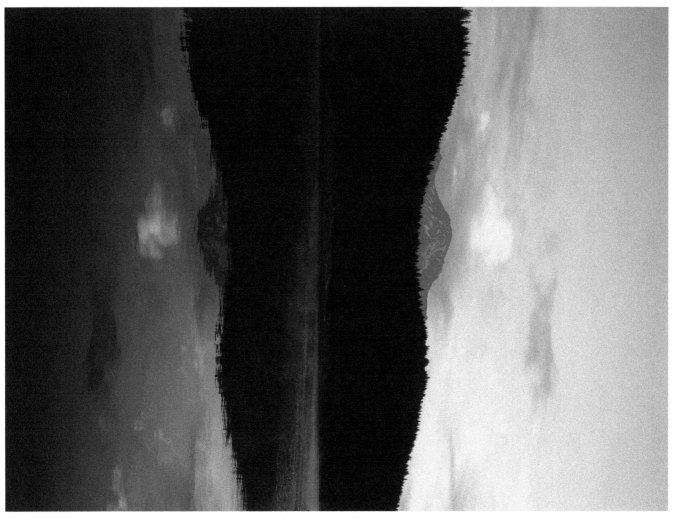

"Sophia reaches down to us".

PLATE 1 CHAPTER 13 was symmetrical when I took it. It was taken at Mount Shasta in Northern California. The mountain is being reflected in Lake Shasta. While I was camping there, I woke up early before the sun came up, and I walked down to the lake. In the twilight in-between time, this was what I saw in my "before completion" time. In nature's symmetry unaltered, I saw through the eyes of my heart center, the divine feminine walking ahead of me. On either side of her, I could see her hands reaching down as if she was offering to take me by the hand.

I was reminded of a passage in the <u>Jerusalem Bible</u> in the book <u>Wisdom</u> 14–17, about Sophia:

> "Watch for her early, and you will not have trouble; you will find her sitting at your gates" "Even to think about her is understanding fully grown; be on the alert for her, and anxiety will quickly leave you. She herself walks about looking for those who are worthy of her, and graciously shows herself to them as they go, in every thought of theirs coming to meet them".

Saint Hildegard of Bingen (1098–1179) said of Sophia that "she is where God stoops to humanity and humanity aspires to God." This is the picture of this symmetrical connection for me.

Mount Shasta has been thought of as one of the global locations around the world that is universally considered a sacred place. It is associated with the throat chakra, which has to do with communication of a higher nature. I felt it was significant that this picture be included near the end of this book because I feel it is not just for me alone, but a communication and an invitation to everyone. Reach up and take her hand. We can't do this alone.

PLATE 2 CHAPTER 13

"Shasta Mountain Mother".

PLATE 2 CHAPTER 13 is another picture, unaltered, of Mount Shasta. Since I do not have it in symmetry, look at it vertically in profile. First, we will look at it with the mountain facing to the right. In profile is the full beautiful figure of the Veiled Great Mother. When we reverse the picture, looking at it vertically with the mountain facing left, we see the head of her divine king son crowned with a cone-shaped crown. Again, this shows the androgynous nature of all life. It also represents the divine feminine as the embodiment of the wisdom of God.

PLATE 3 CHAPTER 13

"His head and her body unaltered".

Here is another example of a picture that shows us his head, and her body or torso that I see so often in profile. **PLATE 3 CHAPTER 13** has been unaltered. You have to look at what you are seeing as if it is in profile. At the top, facing left, is his head, with the snake beside him. In front of him we can see her body is facing inward from the other direction in darker brown. The dove is where her behind would be just above her leg. These pictures are somewhat abstract, but they are everywhere. Perhaps you will also see them on some of your nature walks. Together they represent the yin yang of wholeness of the snake and the dove.

PLATE 4 CHAPTER 13

"In a rural grotto in Italy".

PLATE 4 CHAPTER 13 is another picture taken by Germaine Hammon, in a rural grotto in Italy. It shows the virgin Mary as the one who unites with her wisdom and comfort. In some cultures, she is very much a part of their spiritual life. Beneath her are the people whom she has gathered into her protection. It is another encouraging image of the virgin mother taking care of her own. This must have been experienced by the person who made this piece of pottery to grace this grotto.

There is another side of Sophia that might be considered a more negative side of her archetype. She warns us in the Book of Proverbs, what happens if we do not pay attention to her communication.

Proverbs 1:23 - 28 "Pay attention to my warning:
Now I will pour out my heart to you,
and tell you what I have to say.
Since I have called and you have refused me,
since I have beckoned and no one has taken notice,
since you have ignored all my advice
and rejected all my warnings,
I, for my part, will laugh at your distress,
I will jeer at you when calamity comes,
when calamity bears down on you like a storm
and your distress like a whirlwind,
when disaster and anguish bear down on you.
Then they shall call to me, but I will not answer,
they shall seek me eagerly and shall not find me.

We have to consciously respond to her wisdom when it comes and accept it when it is offered. She is patient, but she can-not be ignored. She speaks in symbols, and from the in-between heart center of our lives. We need to attend.

"Washington National Cathedral".

Back in December 2014, I took a trip to Washington DC. While I was there, I noticed that both the Capitol building, and the Washington National Cathedral had scaffolding around them. It gave the appearance of needing to be repaired or being under reconstruction. I felt it was very symbolic of the state of our country, and it's need for attention both spiritually and governmentally. We have certainly seen our collective torn apart, like the charioteer's horses pulling in opposite directions and it is obvious we have not yet found our center. I see a lot of ego agendas and division but not much self-reflection happening in Washington DC.

The scaffolding around the Washington Cathedral was as the result of an earthquake back in 2011. This is the same year of the Twin Towers disaster in New York City, when we were attacked on 9/11. It seems we got a number of wake-up calls that year, but did we get the message we needed to get?

On this day I entered the cathedral through the east doorway, walking under the scaffolding. The sanctuary had black cloth draped under the ceiling to catch any debris that might fall. It gave the sanctuary a mournful appearance. I was going there as a tourist, and to light candles for my late husband. I wanted to see the beautiful stained-glass windows. I arrived as the service was just beginning, so I sat in the sanctuary and listened.

It was Advent season, so I was expecting something seasonal and traditional. Instead, I was surprised to hear a rip-roaring fire-and-brimstone sermon, warning of impending judgment directed at our nation. We were told not to be surprised at the fallout that could bring us down, and that in fact, we should be watching for it. This was quite a sermon from our nation's Capital Cathedral. I did not know what to make of it. There was no guidance, only dire predictions.

Recently, the bishop of the Catholic cathedral in Washington DC stepped down, because of alleged complacence with pedophile priests who were being indicted from a parish he had previously led. I thought to myself, *that our spiritual leaders seem to be showing us that they are without a North Star direction. It felt like a mournful time of sackcloth and ashes.* It is definitely a time of dismantling and dissolving. As yet, we do not see the healing process beginning. It is a time of painfully, and spiritually hanging out. For some, it could be time to go into your cocoon. For others, it could be a time of chaotic disruption.

In this in-between time, we need to become mindful of our own soul and spirit and do what we can to help others. We take responsibility for what is on our own plate, so others won't have to. It is about standing up for what we know to be sacred, sustaining, and true. There is no more room for denial and maintaining the status quo. We are facing what we have not wanted to face for some time. As a collective, we may need to go through the cleansing fire, even if it reduces some of what we have depended on in the past to ashes.

The alchemist is told not to despise the ash. This is the time when the situation is reduced to its most base common denominator, so that now the process of transformation can begin. From this point, it can be a new beginning.

Carl Jung was often called a wise man or a sage, but his answer to that was, "A man once dipped a hatful of water from a stream, but I do nothing. Other people are at the same stream, but most of them find they have to do something with it. I do nothing. I stand and behold, admiring what nature can do." I think as we enter the age of the "water bearer," we must take this wisdom to heart. Our egos do not need to be always doing; it might be better sometimes to just observe nature and take in the process.

Paradoxically, he writes in retrospect, "the more uncertain I have felt about myself, the more there has grown up in me a feeling of kinship with all things." I too find that the more uncertain I have felt about myself, the more there is a feeling of kinship with nature and all her creatures. I think this would be a good starting point for our inner work.

Jung tells us in his book *Psychology and Alchemy* about how to approach "the work." "The mind must be in harmony with the work, and the work must be above all else." In another passage, he says, "in order to acquire the golden understanding, one must keep the eyes of the mind, and soul well open, observing and contemplating by means of that inner light which God has lit in nature and in our hearts from the beginning." Thank you, Carl Jung, for all you have shared of your work.

If this was a movie instead of a book, there would be two songs that I would play for the ending. I have mentioned songs throughout the book that have accompanied my process and lifted me up. It is so often that we associate songs with the experiences in our life. These final songs are very meaningful to me. They bring tears to my eyes every time I hear them. They are both Stevie Wonder songs.

The first one is called "Black Orchid," from his *Secret Life of Plants* album. This song did not become a hit. I think it was because it was way ahead of its time. I would like to re-visit this song with you because it certainly expresses the Sojourning divine feminine, with hope for a better future. Who better than Stevie Wonder to sing it?

He sings, "She's a pearl of wisdom entrapped by poverty." This is so much like our inner selves that do not know how to become satisfied, because we have left the divine feminine and the inner child behind. This will continue until we can begin to retrieve this divine feminine and her divine child and experience it within ourselves. Until then, we are bereft. He sings, "She gives love with purity, filling minds with hopeful schemes, to build worlds enhanced by peace." At the very end of the song, he sings straight to her. "You know in every heart that beats, you hold a special place." Amen!

The final song is, in my imagination, her reply to us in return. That song is "As" from Stevie Wonder's album *"Songs in the Key of Life"*. He sings, "I'll be loving you, until the day that I am you and you are me. That's always, alwayyyyyys, always." She will be loving us "until mother nature says her work is through." I have to get up and do a little happy dance when I hear this. Go on YouTube and listen to these two songs, sung from the heart by Stevie Wonder.

This is the end, but as they say, "endings bring new beginnings." Amen.

CPSIA information can be obtained
at www.ICGtesting.com
Printed in the USA
BVHW022154270721
613071BV00017B/390